TOXIC EDUCATION
How Schools Are Damaging Young People's Health and Wellbeing and How We Can Fix Them

Chris Bonell

P

First published in Great Britain in 2025 by

Policy Press, an imprint of
Bristol University Press
University of Bristol
1–9 Old Park Hill
Bristol
BS2 8BB
UK
t: +44 (0)117 374 6645
e: bup-info@bristol.ac.uk

Details of international sales and distribution partners are available at policy.bristoluniversitypress.co.uk

© Bristol University Press 2025

British Library Cataloguing in Publication Data
A catalogue record for this book is available from the British Library

ISBN 978-1-4473-7531-9 hardcover
ISBN 978-1-4473-7532-6 paperback
ISBN 978-1-4473-7533-3 ePub
ISBN 978-1-4473-7534-0 ePdf

The right of Chris Bonell to be identified as author of this work has been asserted by him in accordance with the Copyright, Designs and Patents Act 1988.

All rights reserved: no part of this publication may be reproduced, stored in a retrieval system, or transmitted in any form or by any means, electronic, mechanical, photocopying, recording, or otherwise without the prior permission of Bristol University Press.

Every reasonable effort has been made to obtain permission to reproduce copyrighted material. If, however, anyone knows of an oversight, please contact the publisher.

The statements and opinions contained within this publication are solely those of the author and not of the University of Bristol or Bristol University Press. The University of Bristol and Bristol University Press disclaim responsibility for any injury to persons or property resulting from any material published in this publication.

Bristol University Press and Policy Press work to counter discrimination on grounds of gender, race, disability, age and sexuality.

Cover design: Dave Rodgers
Front cover image: iStock/kontrast-fotodesign

For Siwan, Carys and Tom, and in memory of Bethan

Contents

About the author		vi
Acknowledgements		vii
1	Introduction: how schools can seriously damage young people's health	1
2	Toxic experiences: what young people say about schools	6
3	Toxic trends and patterns: data on young people's health	22
4	Toxic policy? Education policy and its consequences	33
5	Health interventions in schools as sticking plasters	42
6	The Learning Together intervention: effective school detox in England	49
7	International examples of effective school detox	68
8	What works, for whom and where	78
9	Detoxifying education policy	87
10	Conclusion: detoxifying education	96
References		100
Index		122

About the author

Chris Bonell is a sociologist and public health researcher who specialises in adolescent health and interventions to improve this. He teaches at the London School of Hygiene & Tropical Medicine and previously worked at the University of Oxford and the Social Exclusion Unit. He provided scientific advice to the UK government and the World Health Organization during the COVID-19 pandemic, and he is a member of the Department for Education Science Advisory Council. He lives in Walthamstow with his partner and two children.

Acknowledgements

Almost everything I have ever written has been co-authored with colleagues. This reflects the fact that the research we do is a collective and collaborative effort. So it feels quite weird to be writing this book alone. The reason I am doing so is because the book not only reports the scientific results of various collaborative research projects but also includes personal experiences and political opinions. It would be too much to ask any co-authors to indulge the former or endorse the latter.

Where I refer to research studies in this book, I often refer to named colleagues where they played a particularly major role in shaping the research or influencing my opinions. But I couldn't name everybody involved in each study. So here I would like to thank all those who have worked with me over the years, providing skills that I lack and perspectives that I have learnt from. Huge thanks go to Elizabeth Allen, Helen Austerberry, Vashti Berry, Leo Bevilacqua, Sarah Jayne Blakemore, Laurence Blanchard, Lyndal Bond, Sara Bragg, Helen Burchett, Rona Campbell, Annah Chollet, Andrew Copas, Steve Cummins, Karen Devries, Matt Dodd, Diana Elbourne, Caroline Farmer, Natasha Fitzgerald-Yau, Adam Fletcher, Ann Hagell, Dan Hale, Angela Harden, Dougal Hargreaves, Lauren Herlitz, Farah Jamal, Anne Johnson, Fraizer Kiff, Rosa Legood, Theo Lorenc, Anne Mathiot, Jennifer McGowan, Rebecca Meiksin, Alec Miners, Graham Moore, Ann Oakley, Charles Opondo, Norren Orr, Amy Peterson, Ruth Ponsford, Pandora Pound, Sidnei Priolo Filho, Tim Rhodes, Emma Rigby, Andrew Rizzo, Kelly Rose-Clarke, Zia Sadique, Mary Sawtell, Stephen Scott, Jeremy Segrott, Nichola Shackleton, Naomi Shaw, Annik Sorhaindo, Vicki Strange, Jo Sturgess, Neisha Sundaram, Tara Tancred, Bruce Taylor, Nerissa Tilouche, Russell Viner, Emily Warren, Helen Weiss, Michael Wigelsworth, Meg Wiggins and Honor Young.

I owe a particularly huge debt to Lyndal Bond, Adam Fletcher, G.J. Melendez Torres, Bo Paulle, Miranda Perry, Vicki Strange and Russell Viner for having a major influence on how I think about schools. Brian Flay, Farah Jamal and George Patton, who are sadly not around anymore and greatly missed, were also huge influences.

I have also hugely benefited from learning about the realities of teaching from friends and relatives who are or were teachers. These include Liz Adshead, Nick Bonell, Zoe Bonell, Daniel Bruton, Gesine Carter, Ruksana Mataria, Miranda Perry, Polly Shields and Michael Whitworth. I have a feeling you won't all agree with all my suggestions though!

I would also like to thank Stephen Collishaw and Tamsin Ford for helping me identify some of the key evidence that has informed this book.

Most of the studies that have informed this book have been funded by the Public Health Research Programme of the National Institute for Health and

Care Research. The intervention costs and evaluation of the educational impacts of the Learning Together intervention were funded by the Education Endowment Foundation. My colleagues and I are grateful for this funding. The views expressed in this book are my own and do not necessarily reflect those of the National Institute for Health and Care Research, the National Health Service, the Department of Health and Social Care for England or the Education Endowment Foundation.

Lastly, I would like to thank all the young people and school staff whom I have worked with and talked to during the various studies reported in this book. Your views are reported anonymously but I am very grateful for your sharing these with me.

1

Introduction: how schools can seriously damage young people's health

Overview of the book

This book is about how secondary schools can seriously damage the health of young people and can continue to affect them as adults. But it is also about how secondary schooling can be modified to avoid this damage and benefit young people's health and learning.

In human evolution and history, schools are a recent innovation and quite a strange one. If brought back to life, prehistoric hunter-gatherers or even medieval merchants would be amazed and probably baffled by our approach to socialising the young by separating them off from everyday society in special institutions, sorting them into classes by age and putting them under the guidance of a single adult at the front of the class. The historical norm for socialising the young was through participating in society, being attached to social groups mixing the old and the young, and learning through observing, copying and improving on what they saw others doing. Schools have developed gradually over the last couple of centuries, with initially only the European White male gentry going to school to prepare to become gentlemen and various sorts of boss. It was not until the second half of the 20th century that secondary schooling became the norm in Europe and North America, and this is only now becoming the norm across the rest of the world.

I am a public health researcher. I explore trends and patterns in young people's health 'outcomes' and 'risk behaviours'. Health outcomes can include adverse outcomes, such as diseases, or positive outcomes, such as wellbeing. Risk behaviours are the actions that can affect health, such as smoking tobacco, engaging in violence and not engaging in physical activity. I examine how schools can affect risk behaviours and health outcomes. I also develop and test 'interventions'. 'Intervention' is the jargon that researchers and policy wonks use to describe purposeful activities aiming to achieve a particular goal – in my case, modifying schools to improve health or reduce risk. Most of my work has been in secondary schools in England, and much of the research I present in this book comes from England and the UK. But I also work in schools in some other countries and the book draws on international evidence. I often focus on the English or UK experience but try to position this within a broader, international perspective. I examine how schools and education policy vary between countries and what this might mean for young people's health. The book focuses overwhelmingly on adolescents and the schools they attend. In most countries, these schools are called secondary or high schools. In some countries, younger adolescents attend middle school before high school. In some poorer countries, adolescents may only get a basic education within extended primary schools.

My argument in this book is that schooling as it is currently commonly undertaken can harm the young via three 'toxic mechanisms'. My understanding of these mechanisms arose from work I did initially with Adam Fletcher and then various other colleagues. The first mechanism involves some young people coming to feel disengaged from education when this does not realistically offer them a way to define a positive sense of their identity and status and their transition to adulthood. In consequence, these young people look to develop alternative ways of defining their identity, status and transition to adulthood through risk behaviours, such as smoking tobacco, drinking alcohol, using drugs, engaging in violence and engaging in early and risky sex. The second mechanism is triggered not by educational disengagement but by the young feeling little sense of belonging or community at school. This can encourage these young people to build a sense of belonging through alternative communities, often in opposition to the formal school culture. This, again, is often facilitated by engaging in risk behaviours, such as violence, drug use and risky sex. The third mechanism is triggered by young people feeling fearful and anxious. They might feel fearful and unsafe because of violence and abuse at school. Or they might feel anxious about schoolwork or exams. In each case, they feel that the school doesn't do enough to support them in dealing with these challenges. These experiences can cause immediate mental distress. They might also cause young people to 'self-medicate' with drugs or alcohol. Or they might cause young people to build protective relationships with the sorts of peers who might otherwise be potential threats, again facilitated by engaging in risk behaviours. All three mechanisms have the potential to increase young people's involvement in risk behaviours and thereby to damage health in adulthood. The mechanisms also have the potential to increase health inequalities because they particularly harm young people from disadvantaged or minoritised backgrounds.

Such harms are not inevitable. Schooling and education have the potential to be enormously beneficial to health and all other aspects of young people's development. Enrolling in school and remaining in school throughout adolescence are important global drivers of better health for adolescents as well as later parenthood and lower mortality and better health, social and economic outcomes in adulthood.[1-3] Being in school can improve health by broadening life choices, improving incomes and protecting young people from exploitation. Across the world, school enrolments are rising but many young people still miss out on the full benefits schooling can bring.[4] The key argument I want to make in this book is that although the quantity of education in the form of enrolments and years of schooling matters for health, so too does the quality of schooling that young people receive. For many students, particularly those from disadvantaged groups, secondary schools can be toxic places.[5]

I have spent most of my career as a public health researcher exploring these mechanisms and what we might do to disrupt them. This book tells the story of this research. Initially, the research that my colleagues and I pursued was focused on understanding what can go wrong. We interviewed young people and teachers to hear their stories. This is called qualitative research. Qualitative research aims to understand people's narratives of their experiences. Qualitative research can also involve researchers observing people's actions. Qualitative research is very good at exploring how people understand the world, what motivates their actions and how they interact with others. It provides a fine-grained view, which allows us to develop theories about how things happen.

Although qualitative research is good at developing theories, it generally involves quite small samples and is less good at mapping broader patterns. It is not so strong at testing whether the theories we develop apply more generally. So, my colleagues and I have also conducted surveys to measure young people's disengagement from education and lack of support, and how these are associated with various risk behaviours and health outcomes. This led some who read this research to see me as an implacable opponent of conventional schools and schooling, and therefore not to be trusted. I remember one senior civil servant who suggested that I should not receive government funding for research because of my bizarre views. This was a surprise to me because education and learning have always been at the centre of my life. As a child, educated in a tough comprehensive in the English Midlands, I didn't always enjoy school but I was always deeply in love with learning for its own sake and as a passport to a better life.

Later on, the research that I and my colleagues pursued became more focused on developing and evaluating interventions to address the problems we had earlier identified. These interventions consisted of activities to change schools to improve young people's engagement, belonging and support with the aim of preventing risk behaviours, such as violence and drug use, and promoting positive outcomes, such as good mental health. We have used various experimental and quasi-experimental methods to examine what impacts these interventions have. This terminology is explained in Chapter 6. We have found from our own studies, as well as those conducted by others, that such interventions really can reduce risk behaviours, benefit health and improve educational attainment. In addition to helping to improve my reputation with civil servants, the evaluations of these interventions have demonstrated that the toxic mechanisms described earlier are not an inevitable part of secondary schooling. We discovered that it is perfectly possible for schools to take relatively simple steps to disrupt these toxic mechanisms and thereby improve the health as well as the educational attainment of their students.

That schools can be beneficial to students was underlined to me and many others by what happened to young people during the COVID-19 pandemic. I was one of the scientists brought in to inform government policy. I began this work in March 2020, helping advise on how school closures should occur while supporting the most vulnerable students. I was then involved in many discussions about when and how schools could re-open safely. With colleagues, I initiated and helped lead a study examining COVID-19 transmissions in schools and the feasibility and impact of the measures that schools took to minimise transmission. I was one of a group of researchers, led by Russell Viner, who made the case that infections among young people were unlikely to be the most important driver of the pandemic and that schools should re-open as quickly as possible to curtail the harms to young people's education, social development and wellbeing that closures generated. As the pandemic receded, I was one of a group of researchers who argued that schools needed to 'build back better', focusing on students' wellbeing and educational attainment as complementary, not competing, goals.

The book also explores how, in the UK and elsewhere, the toxic mechanisms that can harm young people's health are likely to be unintentional consequences of some government education policies. In many countries, schools have become largely self-managing but operate within the context of a national curriculum, a schools inspectorate and school performance league tables, which aim to ensure schools operate at a high standard. I explore how this type of system, on the one hand, has brought some benefits in terms of efficient school management and consistency of standards but, on the other hand, has pump-primed the toxic mechanisms described earlier.

The book explores how education policy might be modified to help disrupt these toxic mechanisms. What I recommend is not the complete dismantling of the system of school autonomy, standards and accountability. Research suggests that doing so can often make the problem worse. The current system is quite effective in encouraging schools to achieve certain outputs and outcomes; it is just that these are very often the wrong sorts of outputs and outcomes. The book describes how this problem might be solved by adjusting rather than completely dismantling the current system. It considers some possible changes – for example, in what is taught, what teaching methods are used and the status of the teaching profession – to improve the education and the health of young people.

Who might read this book

I hope that this book will be of interest to teachers thinking about how their schools can better support students' wellbeing and learning using practical, feasible actions. I hope it will also be of interest to young people and parents who are interested in how things can go so wrong in schools and what they might demand of schools and education policies to remedy this. I hope it will be of interest to education policy makers who are interested in making education systems less toxic without tearing down the entire system and starting again. And I hope it will be of interest to public health researchers interested in effective and sustainable actions to improve the health of young people and the adults they become.

2

Toxic experiences: what young people say about schools

Introduction

This chapter describes the toxic mechanisms that occur in secondary schools which can harm young people's health. The chapter draws mainly on qualitative research to explore three toxic mechanisms as they are experienced by students. Some of this qualitative research has been done by me and my colleagues. Some of it has been done by other researchers. As explained at the start of this book, qualitative research draws on interviews, focus groups and observations to try to understand how people experience the world. Interviews and focus groups involve researchers asking open-ended questions and then listening to people's stories in their own words. Qualitative research explores people's accounts of their experiences and the meanings they give to these as well as how they act and interact with others. It can explore how people's actions can be enabled and constrained by the institutions within which they find themselves (such as schools). And it can explore the immediate consequences of their actions.

Qualitative research is strong on understanding the details of social processes and how these are experienced by people. It can help us develop theories about cause and effect in the lives of people and across society.[6] Qualitative research is less strong on testing the wider applicability of these theories. It generally draws on small samples of participants and contexts. It doesn't collect exactly the same sorts of data from each participant. And it generally does not track people for long periods of time. While the participants involved in qualitative research often have clear insights into the immediate context for and consequences of their actions, they may not see everything. They are less likely to see the more 'upstream' factors, which affect their actions, or the more 'downstream', long-term consequences of these actions. For this reason, the theories that emerge from qualitative research should, where possible, be tested using quantitative research involving larger samples of people, more standardised data and longer periods of follow-up. This lets us see whether the patterns of statistical associations in these broader data support our theories. I do that in later chapters. But in this chapter, I mainly focus on qualitative research, examining each of the three toxic mechanisms.

Toxic disengagement

The first mechanism involves educational disengagement. Research done by psychologists and cognitive neuroscientists suggests that as adolescents progress through secondary school, they increasingly seek to establish a sense of their own autonomy and personal identity.[7,8] They want to assert more independence from their families and develop their own sense of who they are. This will be bound up with ideas about their social status and their transition to adulthood. The precise markers of identity, social status and transition to adulthood will vary between historical periods and cultural groups, but the same fundamental process occur in most places.

Some students develop a strong sense of who they are through engaging with learning and doing well academically in schools. Schools can offer such engaged students very positive markers of identity, status and transition to adulthood. I vividly remember the positive way in which academic learning, and doing well in tests and examinations, fed into my own sense of self. I was from a working-class community and a family where no one had gone to university, and school helped me develop my identity as someone with a love of science and literature. It gave me the status of successful student. And it gave me a belief that my transition to adulthood would involve going to university and having a successful career. However, this is not the experience of all students, and many of my schoolmates did not experience this. Schools can be experienced as toxic when students feel that they cannot achieve these 'pro-school' markers.[9] Some of this may be down to the students and their varying capacities and ambitions, but much of it is down to schools. It is much more likely to happen in schools where students are turned off learning by a narrow curriculum or unengaging teaching methods.[5] It is much more likely to affect students from socially disadvantaged backgrounds. Some disadvantaged students may not have been brought up to regard educational engagement as the default. And some may not possess the cultural or economic resources that are useful in supporting learning;[10] the former might include the cultural skills to interact with middle-class teachers, while the latter might include an adequate space for homework.

Stories of disengagement

Together with my colleague Adam Fletcher, I explored this phenomenon in qualitative research with some educationally disengaged students in Park Grove school in London (to ensure confidentiality, real school names are not used).[11] Overall, the school had a track record of strong student performance in academic examinations. However, our interviews with a group of White British, female students, who described themselves as the 'hyper girls', highlighted how some students felt unable to get with this programme. This was partly because they felt they could not meet the academic demands of the school. It was also because many of these girls, who came from poor and sometimes chaotic families, felt unable to take on the passive, childlike role of learner that the school expected of them. As one of these girls commented: 'I've had to be an adult for, like, my whole life really. But oh no, they just think they always know best 'cos they are the teacher and we are the students. And we've gotta listen to them' (p 555).[11]

The hyper girls felt disengaged from, and actively scorned, the school's emphasis on academic attainment. As one of them described:

> [The head teacher] wants the perfect school. In assembly, all she talks about is 'Our school is in the newspaper. We are the perfect school. Blah, blah.' That's all she wants – the perfect school … exam marks, how tidy the school is. It's not her doing it! It's us doing it! But she doesn't give any credit for it. I can walk round school with my tie undone, my shirt out and that. Yeah, I'd get in trouble but I can do what I wanna do. (p 555)[11]

Such educational disengagement is more likely in schools where the narrowness of the curriculum offers only a very limited number of ways to be a good student, which will not align with some students' aptitudes or interests.[10,12] It can also happen when staff project low expectations or offer low levels of support to some students, such as those from working-class or minoritised communities.[5,13] Streaming and setting, whereby students spend all or some of their time in classes stratified by academic ability, can also feed into these processes. At Park Grove, for example, one hyper girl described how the practice of placing the most disengaged students together in a low-ability set reinforced their disengagement: 'Everyone in the bottom sets, they are all the naughty people. I'm with every other naughty person and it's not a good combination of people for the teachers!' (p 555).[11]

Disengagement harming health

How, then, might this mechanism of disengagement harm health? Our own and others' qualitative research suggests that feeling unable to build a sense of identity, status and transition to adulthood through educational engagement can encourage some students to engage in certain 'street styles' to find alternative markers for these.[13–15] Enacting street styles often includes enacting repertoires of risk behaviours, such as smoking tobacco or cannabis, drinking alcohol, using other drugs, engaging in violence[5,13] or initiating early sexual activity.[9,16] There is evidence that drug use and other risk behaviours have become central to how some marginalised young people construct their cultural identity[17,18] in a context of the erosion of more traditional class-based identities.[19]

A famous study by Paul Willis of disengagement in secondary schools in the English Midlands in the 1970s found that many young working-class men rejected the middle-class school culture centred on learning. They rebelled against this culture by messing about in lessons. Their sense of themselves as working class was overt. A consequence of their active rejection of learning was that these young men had little choice but to take the same sorts of jobs in manufacturing industry as their fathers. Willis drew conclusions from his study about how class inequalities can get replicated from generation to generation not through people being the passive objects of social forces but through their very engagement in small acts of rebellion informed by their class identities.[14] It is hard to imagine the same sorts of findings in a study today. Although class inequalities remain, class-based identities are less clear. Young men and women may still react against school cultures focused on academic learning and attainment with which they do not feel they can engage. But their rebellions are much more likely to be imbued with street styles and associated risk behaviours, such as drug use and violence, rather than with traditional class identities.

Our research at Park Grove illustrates some of these processes. For the disengaged hyper girls, drug use could be an important means of constructing their individual and collective identity. As one of them explained: 'We all meet up at like eight o'clock [near school], smoke a zute [cannabis joint], then go down the shop for the munchies. Then we'd go in school absolutely bollocksed!' (p 556).[11]

Using tobacco, alcohol or other drugs could also offer a marker of the transition to adulthood. This could enable them to look and feel 'adult'. In the context of a highly controlled and academic school environment, drug use offered these students a more subtle and less challengeable way to resist the dominant school culture than might other behaviours, such as violence or other overtly rebellious behaviour, as some of the hyper girls alluded to: 'I'm more mellow now … I'm like "Stop shouting at me, man, chill out!"'; 'When you're stoned, you either just ignore the teachers or crack up!' (p 557)[11] Other research has pointed to how early involvement in relationships and sex can similarly offer a marker of the transition to adulthood for some students.[20]

At Park Grove, being 'stoned' also provided the hyper girls with an excuse for their educational failure. As some of the girls explained:

It makes me slow and I get dozy from blazing [smoking cannabis]. I can't do my work then! (p 557)[11]

When you're chilled before school, you're just like really tired and everything is a blur and you're not concentrating on the work.

> Everyone who is normal can concentrate and answer questions and stuff ... when you're stoned and the teacher asks you a question, you either crack up laughing or just start stuttering and everything [but] when you're normal, you're on the ball. (p 557)[11]

Together with Farah Jamal and Angela Harden, I conducted a review of the broader qualitative research on how schools might influence health. Farah was a wonderful researcher and a delightful person who shockingly and sadly died way too young. One of Farah's many insights was her theory that for some students in some schools, there are parallel systems of learning, discipline and community. There is the official system run by the school, focused on academic attainment and good behaviour. Then there is the unofficial system run by students, focused on the learning of street styles and risk behaviours.[21]

Disengagement from school can encourage some young people to engage in risk behaviours, such as drug use or early sexual activity, because these provide alternative markers of identity, status and transition to adulthood. For other students, being disengaged from education might simply mean that there is less reason for them not to engage in these behaviours. Most educationally engaged students will avoid use of tobacco, alcohol or drugs, early sexual activity and pregnancy, and violence because these are likely to act as barriers to success at school and routes into higher education or careers. Educationally disengaged students are likely to have lower expectations about their future education and career and so be less likely to see the need to avoid these risk behaviours.[22,23] For example, Lisa Arai's qualitative research about young people's sexual and pregnancy decision-making suggests that for educationally disengaged young women, early pregnancy might not be viewed negatively as a barrier to education and might be viewed as a positive outcome. There might be less reason to opt to terminate a pregnancy.[20] Qualitative research from California, US, with young Latina and White women suggests that for many of these young women, a lack of belief in them on the part of teachers could feed into their seeing no reason not to get pregnant, as was apparent in one interview:

> Even as she voiced ... plans [to become a social worker], Juliana pointed out, more than once, that she was 'a troublemaker', observing that (white middle class) teachers at Morton had described her this way ... I asked her where she thought she would be in five years. 'Probably pregnant!' she said. 'Everybody thinks I'm going to get pregnant.' (p 398)[24]

In contrast, for young women from more advantaged backgrounds, educational goals are achieved partly via strategies of avoiding sex, using contraception or having abortions.[23]

Toxic lack of belonging

The second mechanism is triggered not by young people feeling disengaged from learning, but rather by them lacking a sense of belonging in the school community. It is easy to view the past overly positively, but there is evidence that societies have undergone shifts in the last few decades from life being experienced collectively to life being experienced more individually. In the past, neighbours were often also workmates, and there was limited residential and occupational churn. Leisure activities were often collective, based around local clubs. Since the 1980s, there have been increases in residential and occupational mobility, a decline in employment in large industries employing a whole town, and a rise in individual leisure. The US social scientist Robert Putnam offers, as an example of this, the transition from Americans participating in ten-pin bowling in local clubs to 'bowling alone'.[25]

In the realm of education, social scientists have highlighted the increasing individualisation of the transition from education to work, the risks associated with this and the consequent intensification of individuals striving for qualifications.[19] Whereas, previously, entire cohorts of young people would move from school into factories and other large enterprises, increasingly transitions are more extended and diverse. A similar process of individualisation can occur in the experience of being schooled, despite schools obviously being institutions that collect young people together. Our sense from having done multiple projects in schools is that modern schools can sometimes feel less like real communities and more like battery farms for promoting individual academic progress. Each student is monitored in terms of their performance in repeated tests as well as in terms of their behaviour. The results are fed back individually so that trends can be identified and the necessary actions taken to maximise performance in public examinations. This process of individualisation is exacerbated as a result of the reduction in collective activities in schools, such as sports, drama and assemblies, because of budget cuts or to find more time for learning.

Qualitative research on lack of school belonging

Schools should be communities that value diversity and at the same time offer a sense of belonging. But schools can be toxic when students feel little sense of belonging in a real community. We did a review of qualitative research on how school environments can influence health. This suggests that poor relationships between staff and students can be a major aspect of this lack of a sense of belonging in a school community. This is particularly so when students perceive interactions with teachers as being purely instrumental in nature, focused on academic performance, and lacking affective dimensions or a focus on the whole student.[21] Qualitative studies also suggest that students' sense of belonging in school can be eroded when they feel they have little say in how schools are run.[21] Some qualitative studies suggest that students lacking a sense of belonging may engage in overt resistance to school cultures that they experience as excluding or marginalising – in terms of race and ethnicity, for example.[13,14,26]

Lack of belonging harming health

Feeling little sense of belonging in a school community can harm health in several different ways. Given the research evidence of the association between social connection and mental wellbeing[27] and the evidence that the need for belonging is particularly heightened among adolescents,[28] lack of school belonging might directly harm mental health. A lack of sense of school belonging might also encourage students to develop an alternative sense of belonging through their participation in anti-school peer groups facilitated by engagement in risk. Adam Fletcher and I conducted qualitative research in Highbridge School, a mixed-sex comprehensive school in London with a highly disadvantaged intake. This included an interview with Sabrina (all participant names are pseudonyms), who had avoided becoming embroiled in anti-school groups and instead engaged in extracurricular activities, through which she had developed a strong sense of school belonging. As a young woman of African Caribbean heritage, Sabrina embraced aspects of Black street culture and dialect, but she also described how she had good relationships with some teachers and some of the more pro-school students. She explained that she was 'sweet' (had good relationships) with the 'little miss girlies and the other White chicks' (p 247).[29] Sabrina's involvement in extracurricular sessions may have enabled her to form these bonds with teachers and with 'sweet' 'groups' of students, helping build her sense of school belonging:

Interviewer:	Do you feel like a part of this school?
Sabrina:	Yeah. I always after school do stuff. I used to do a lot of sports but that was when I was in year seven and eight [age 11–13 years] I stopped that now. I still do cooking and kickboxing, mentoring. And the teacher takes us jogging if you get here early and that was actually good but the food weren't! You meet lots of people though.
Interviewer:	Do you find it useful to be involved with all this extra stuff?
Sabrina:	Yeah, very. (p 248)[29]

This involvement appeared to have enabled Sabrina to develop good relationships with staff at the school. She explained that she was 'bless' (got on well) with teachers and would 'talk to them and have jokes with them' after school (p 248).[29] She avoided smoking 'weed' (cannabis), drinking and other drug use because she prioritised her sense of belonging in this community. However, students lacking this sense of school belonging are less likely to build good relationships with teachers or with pro-school students and more likely to engage in anti-school peer groups as a way to develop an alternative form of community. Our review of qualitative research by other researchers suggests that this forging of alternative communities could often be facilitated by smoking tobacco or cannabis and engaging in violence and other antisocial behaviour.[21]

Toxic fear and anxiety

The third mechanism involves schools failing to support students who are having to deal with fear and anxiety. Schools should offer students an environment in which they feel safe. The sociologist Bowen Paulle conducted observations and interviews in two schools, in New York and Amsterdam, where he worked as a teacher. Both schools were in poor, ethnically diverse and tough neighbourhoods and had many problems with staffing and management. Paulle describes how students could experience these schools as highly toxic as a result of feeling unsafe and anxious.[5] He vividly describes students experiencing chronic stress as a result of a chaotic and often threatening school environment, and how this could result in impaired concentration, disproportionate reactions to social challenges and an eroded sense of wellbeing. Such toxicity can occur when schools fail to establish or enforce norms of orderly and peaceful behaviour so that physical and verbal bullying, sexual harassment, gender-based violence and other violence and abuse are common.[5] We know from survey research that in many secondary schools in England, students feel unsafe.[30]

Stories of fear and anxiety

During our fieldwork at Highbridge School, it was clear to Adam Fletcher and me that many students were anxious about violence and antisocial behaviour in school. A recurring theme was that school was a dangerous place. As one student commented: 'It's scary. You've gotta stand up for yourself – make your name, make friends. If you got friends then at least you know you're safe. Not being the person alone is important. You don't want to be one person alone' (p 245).[29] This was confirmed by interviews with teachers:

> There are elements to it that can be quite rough and frightening, especially if you're a small child in year seven [entry at age 11 or 12]. I could imagine them being terrified. (p 245)[29]

> I'm sure they do have to fall into some sort of grouping in school. I think school does really, by its very nature, divide people up because it's such a big scary place and students need safety in numbers. (p 129)[31]

Other qualitative research describes students having similar experiences with abuse specifically related to gender and sexual orientation. Farah Jamal, Angela Harden and I conducted qualitative research with students at two secondary schools, Eastgrove and Crescent, in London.[32] Both schools were ethnically diverse, with African Caribbean and African students forming the largest groups of students in Eastgrove and most students being of South Asian heritage in Crescent. Eastgrove had an all-girls main campus and a separate mixed-sex centre for girls and boys. Crescent was an all-girls school. Girls in Eastgrove told us that sexual harassment of girls by boys was common. As one girl described: 'One time, I was even in my classroom and two lads came up to me and started like "hey babe, do you want to be my bitch[?]" and things like that … It can happen everywhere' (p 736).[32]

This research also found that gender-based harassment could occur among girls. Girls in both schools reported bullying practices, such as spreading rumours, name-calling and teasing relating to girls' sexuality. As one girl at Crescent described in a focus group: 'They gossip, they spread rumours, they make fun of what music you listen to. And, seriously, I was called a lesbian because I did not find One Direction [boy band] attractive' (p 735).[32] Homophobic insults, such as being called a lesbian, were considered by these girls to be particularly threatening and, as one girl from Crescent reported, could 'ruin your reputation' (p 735).[32]

The toxic mechanism of fear and anxiety related to a lack of safety at school was also apparent to us when we conducted our review of qualitative research on how schools might influence health.[21] Studies we reviewed reported that certain unsupervised school spaces could become unsafe 'hot spots' that were 'unowned' by the formal institution.[33] Our synthesis suggests that these spaces arose particularly when teachers narrowed their role to focus almost exclusively on classroom teaching rather than involvement in and supervision of the wider school site. Teachers considered the latter to be beyond their professional responsibility and often also found them personally intimidating.[34] One female student in a US high school was cited in a qualitative study as follows: 'If there is a fight in the hall, there's no teacher there, and if there's a classroom right next to it …. It's amazing how they don't hear it. When they come out, they just, like, stand there' (p 329).[34]

Our review of qualitative research found further evidence that teachers were increasingly focused narrowly on the educational aspects of school life, often delegating student discipline and pastoral care to other staff, such as security guards, pastoral managers or even on-site police officers.[21] The qualitative research reported that this could feed into student anxiety when these other professionals were perceived as less effective in dealing with disciplinary and pastoral issues. Students reported that behaviour problems were much more likely to be effectively addressed or prevented by teachers viewed as 'caring' or 'respectful', if they were available. Such caring teachers were said to be those who did not confine their role to classroom teaching and were committed to supporting the whole child. One such teacher in a US high school was quoted in a study thus: 'I would say that it is more like parenting. I talk to them [the students]. I don't keep my distance. I do not keep professionalism between us. I say what I really think, how I really feel. I break all of the rules' (p 25).[33]

The research in London schools led by Farah Jamal identified examples of schools responding inadequately to sexual harassment.[32] For example, one girl at Eastgrove told us: 'if someone came up and slapped your bum or whatever or would … [say], like, "oh, your boobs look nice" or whatever, they [the school] would just say it is the norm, because that is what boys are like and stuff like that' (p 736).[32] Another girl at Eastgrove told us that when she reported experiencing sexual harassment to a female teacher, no action was taken. The teacher recognised that the incident had been sexual abuse but, instead of challenging it, advised that the student needed to 'get used to it': 'She says that I will get used to it but she says it in a way that I have to watch [out for] myself. She has to watch herself. And that is what she is saying. If she has to watch herself, then I definitely have to watch myself' (p 736).[32]

Schools appeared to be particularly poor in responding to the sexual harassment of girls by girls. It appeared that despite policies indicating that all sexual harassment would be addressed, teachers often took no action on harassment among girls. As one girl at Crescent commented: 'It should not be happening in the school. And if you try to report a sexual harassment, the teachers do not take it serious, because it's not a boy doing it' (p 735).[32] Echoing the finding from our review of qualitative research reported earlier, according to some girls in a focus group at Crescent, a factor explaining the generally poor response of schools to various forms of sexual harassment was teachers' narrow focus on preparing students for examinations and assessments: 'Even when they find out [about an incident of sexual abuse between girls], they don't take [it] as something very important. As long as the grades are good and the reputation is good, that is enough for them' (p 740).[32]

As well as fear of violence, another source of anxiety is schoolwork and fear of failure. In her book *Toxic Childhood*, Sue Palmer argues that increasingly competitive schools are harming the mental health of their students.[35]

Our own research has explored the mechanisms by which anxiety about academic work can harm the mental and physical health of young people. Students can become anxious when schools fail to support them through learning and assessment.[36] In many schools, assessments come to dominate the educational experience and there is insufficient support for students to cope with these demands.[36] This is exemplified in an interview, carried out as part of another one of our studies, with a student at Southborough, a school in south-east England serving mostly White students:

> I'd say that 'cos I'm in an express group, like, the highest group, they think, 'Oh, you're a top class, you should be getting this'. Like, [grade] sixes in my maths. And yeah it makes me feel nervous 'cos if I don't, I might, like, disappoint them. And they might not think as much of me. (p e24)[24]

Fear and anxiety harming health

Direct impacts

How then might this mechanism of feeling anxious and fearful lead to health harms? One way is that feeling unsafe and anxious can directly harm mental health. Bowen Paulle's qualitative research in schools in disadvantaged areas of New York and Amsterdam found that schools characterised by constant low-level aggression could harm students' mental health through chronic stress.[5] This direct impact was also apparent in qualitative research I conducted with Rebecca Meiksin on girls' experiences of sexual harassment in English secondary schools in southern England. This found that boys' verbal abuse of girls could arouse anxiety and affect girls' confidence. As one girl described:

> I think it lowers their self-esteem kind of, even if it doesn't make it visible or something, it does lower it. Like it is kind of sad because some girls will stop doing, like, stop being confident ... just because they got called this or that, and then they just feel insecure and stuff.

Verbal abuse focused on sexuality could also play a role in regulating and damaging same-sex friendships. As one girl explained: 'Or if, let's say, two girls, say, like, really close friends, and they're always hugging, they'll like call them "lesbian" or [say] "You're a queer" or something like that. Like if you're holding hands with a girl, like, it's like ....'

Safety but also risk in numbers

Adam Fletcher's research in Elmhurst, a London school with low overall academic attainment, suggests another way in which fear of violence and abuse can damage students' health. Students who feel unsafe might strategically engage in risk behaviours, such as drug use or violence, in order to build protective affiliations with peers who might otherwise be threats, but can become sources of protection. One girl described this as follows: 'You have to pretend to be naughty. You have to be naughty to get on with all the naughty kids' (p E24).[22]

This part of the mechanism was also apparent from Adam's interviews with students at Highbridge school. Two young Black men at the school, Jermaine and Kyle, described 'bare [lots of] beefs [conflicts]' at the school (p 246).[29] A recurring theme in interviews with these young men was the importance of being 'safe'. Both described how they projected street styles and tough appearances as a way to stay 'safe' and be 'cool' with as many students in the school as possible. They described how for some students at the school, such styles could extend to being involved in violence. Kyle described how belonging to a 'crew' [group] was regarded as essential to staying safe at school:

Interviewer:	What do you think about gang violence?
Kyle:	It's all political innit? Some people show other people. Other people do it for safety.
Interviewer:	Would you carry a knife?
Kyle:	Yeah, for safety maybe. But I don't go round shanking [stabbing] people, threatening people and all that. (p 246)[29]

Jermaine's and Kyle's accounts made clear that 'blazing' (smoking cannabis) was another way to facilitate membership of a protective social group. Similar mechanisms were apparent at Highbridge among female students. Leanne had recently returned from being excluded from school. She strongly identified with other 'safe' anti-school Black students. Leanne reported how she felt safe because of her membership of a 'crew':

Interviewer:	So a lot of people don't feel safe here you reckon?
Leanne:	Not that many. I'm not being racist or anything but I know for a fact that all the Black kids feel safe.
Interviewer:	Why's that?
Leanne:	They just stick with each other. And if there's a fight they all just jump and stick with their crew.
Interviewer:	It's the White kids who aren't safe?
Leanne:	Well, some other White kids hang with the Black kids 'cos then they know all the big Black kids will fight for them. (p 247)[29]

Leanne said she regularly smoked 'weed' after school. She suggested that a key factor was a desire to look 'bad' and build relationships with other 'safe' kids:

Interviewer:	So why do you all do [smoke cannabis] then?
Leanne:	Well, some people say it keeps you out of trouble. Others say they do it 'cos it makes them more confident. That's what some of 'em told me.
Interviewer:	Is that why you started then?
Leanne:	Er, you smoke it for fun. And you wanna look bad. People think you're bad boy or bad girl.
Interviewer:	What sort of students here smoke cannabis then – what are they like at school?
Leanne:	With me they are cool and I'm safe with the boys here […] but we are the bad ones, the rude ones – get excluded and that. (p 247)[29]

We found similar findings related to this mechanism when we reviewed broader research on the topic.[21] One study of a tough US high school explored how students could engage in violence at unsafe schools as a form of group performance through which norms of acting 'tough' are collectively enacted and a sense of group membership forged. As a researcher observed:

> [They] were throwing punches at each other, trying to push each other's head against the floor with all the strength that they could muster as they twisted their bodies together like twine. They were encircled by a ring of students locked arm in arm as they chanted in unison to the rhythm of the fighters. (p 51)[37]

Other, more engaged students might also smoke cannabis as a strategy to build membership in 'safe' school groups. Roxy was a young Black woman who lived with her mother in an inner London council estate. She described how she was 'aiming high' educationally. She felt 'cool' and 'safe' with the anti-school Black girls, who included Leanne. She avoided being identified with those 'proper good people' who got 'targeted', describing how 'you have to change' to make it safely through secondary school:

Interviewer:	When did you first smoke weed then?
Roxy:	When I was year nine [aged 13–14] … [i]t's the year when everyone messes about after SATs [public exams] and that.
Interviewer:	Where did you get it from then?
Roxy:	Just my friends. You can buy it like. I know a lot people who shot [sell cannabis]. Most people I know do it.
Interviewer:	What sell it or smoke it?
Roxy:	Some of them both. I know at least ten people who deal cannabis.

Interviewer:	At this school?
Roxy:	Some at school yeah, some outside …
Interviewer:	Do you think there are lots of students here smoking weed?
Roxy:	Yeah – it's seen as acceptable like. (p 247)[29]

Some more academic students feel the need to actively perform school disengagement as a means of preserving their protective 'safe' identity. This was described to us in an interview with a teacher at Woodbridge, a comprehensive school in outer London largely serving White students, in another one of our studies:

> This lad, he's known as one of the cool gang, he came up to me and he asked 'Are you sure, I'm meant to be [in the higher academic stream] sir. I should be a little bit lower'. It's just about losing face, and we have quite a few students that have that, kind of, attitude really, they're more about their appearance or what happens outside of school. And the gang, kind of, culture really, 'cos there's quite a few little gangs around the school. (p e24)[22]

Our own research suggests that embracing a 'safe' identity could lead to a vicious circle in which 'fitting in' with 'safe groups' could exacerbate difficult relationships with teachers and, in turn, lead to more cannabis use. As one teacher at Highbridge described:

> The boys seem to just drift into one group or another and then you get categorised. Then you can't be yourself, you follow the group …. Some groups are so heavily involved in and identified by things like drugs that it would be harder to step back from those things. (p 129)[31]

Self-harm and self-medication

There are other ways in which the toxic mechanism of fear and anxiety can damage young people's health. Our research found examples of some students using self-harm, such as cutting the skin on one's arms, as a means of managing anxiety caused by worries about schoolwork.[38] Some students self-medicated with cannabis and other drugs to cope with stress and anxiety. In Adam Fletcher's interviews at Highbridge, 'weed' and 'pills' were repeatedly described by students as a 'cheap [way] to get away from things', such as worries about schoolwork and exams (p 247).[29] One teacher described how it was common for students, including those considered to be 'one of the better ones', to be caught using drugs:

One girl was caught recently sniffing solvents by her parents at home and she was the last person you would expect. People think you know which ones will be your future drug dealers and how many will do coke. With her, it was pressure, pure and simple, she had a lot of expectations on her, from herself, her parents, the school and she had to find somewhere to escape it. She obviously couldn't raise it with anyone else so she dealt with herself by getting high – this was going on for a long time we now know. This wasn't done with groups of friends – it was an outlet to alleviate pressure. (p 247)[29]

This was also apparent in Adam's interviews at Park Grove, where students self-medicated with cannabis to deal with family and school stressors.[11] This included Jaz, one of the White, working-class 'hyper girls' mentioned earlier:

Jaz:	Most people who work [at school], they probably go in and it's all nice. They've probably got a mum and dad and a brother and a sister and dog and nice house, nice car. [...] Your background is what was you before this. Taking drugs makes you feel better.
Interviewer:	Can it make you feel better about school?
Jaz:	Yeah if someone can't be bothered about school, like you're having a bad day then just have a spliff in the morning then it's a good day. Pressure and stress can make people take drugs. [...] If people don't like the environment they're in, they are not going to be comfortable and getting on at school. (p 558)[11]

Avoiding dangerous spaces

Feeling unsafe in certain spaces could also put students off having school meals. Several of the qualitative studies we reviewed reported how some teachers did not use school canteens because they wanted to take a break from students and prepare for lessons. This was said to result in dining halls being insufficiently regulated, meaning that many students avoided these spaces, with implications for whether or not they ate a healthy lunch option.[39][40] In contrast, some studies suggested there were benefits where schools did encourage staff to have lunch with students. Students and teachers in one UK secondary school were said to value time they spent together other than in the classroom. One teacher explained:

Well, when I'm having lunch with the kids, if I'm sitting with them, erm, it's nice, cos I ask them what they're doing at the weekend or if they did anything nice at the weekend or if it's a Monday, erm, what their plans are … I just chat to them like, just a bit more friendly, I suppose … . It's nice, cos they can chat about stuff and they can ask you things. They don't normally get that time, that's not me trying to pump them full of information, so, you know, and it's just a little bit more relaxed. (p 57)[41]

Conclusion

This chapter described multiple ways in which schools can inadvertently harm their students through the mechanisms of educational disengagement, lack of belonging in a school community, and fear and anxiety. Different mechanisms of harm will be more salient in different contexts and with different populations. They may also be expressed in different ways in different contexts. The mechanisms of school disengagement and lack of belonging might involve overt resistance based on class alienation, and this is more likely in societies that retain a strong manufacturing base and overt class structure.[14,19] More passive disengagement might be more likely in post-manufacturing economies with less overt class structures.[11] Lack of belonging might be more likely in heterogeneous populations where there has been limited integration. With the mechanism of fear and anxiety, lack of physical safety may be most likely in violent settings where schools fail to impose order.[5] Anxiety may be most likely in higher-attaining, pressurised schools, especially for girls experiencing pressure to conform or attain.[30]

This chapter reviewed qualitative research to develop an understanding of the toxic mechanisms by which schools might harm their students. The next chapter reviews quantitative evidence to see if this supports these qualitative findings about the role of these mechanisms in generating harmful outcomes.

3

Toxic trends and patterns: data on young people's health

Introduction

The previous chapter described the three toxic mechanisms through which secondary schools might harm student health: educational disengagement; lack of school belonging; and fear and anxiety. The identification of these mechanisms was informed by qualitative research, some of it carried out by me and my colleagues in English secondary schools and some by other author researchers around the world. This qualitative research provides rich insights into the lives of young people and their teachers, how young people understand their place in schools and how this is implicated in some of their decisions, including their decisions to become involved in various risk behaviours. These compelling stories allowed us to develop a detailed understanding of the mechanisms by which schools might harm some students' health. However, it would be hard to conclude from these stories alone that English secondary schools have measurable impacts on the health of their students, or whether such effects also occur in other countries. So in this chapter, I examine quantitative, statistical evidence from the UK and beyond to see whether this supports the existence of worrying trends in young people's health, the possibility of school effects on health and the presence of the three toxic mechanisms.

Young people's health and risk behaviours

The first set of quantitative evidence I briefly review is evidence about trends and patterns in young people's health and risk behaviours. This doesn't provide direct evidence about whether schools influence risk or health, but it does provide useful background to understand how bad the picture is for different areas of health and for different groups of young people. If young people's health is overwhelmingly good, then we might not be very concerned about school effects. But if the picture is bad, then we should be concerned about what role schools are playing in this. If the picture varies for different areas of health and risk, then we should be most interested in school effects in those areas where there are larger problems.

The pattern of adolescent health is complex, with different trends and vulnerabilities for different areas of mental and physical health and different groups of young people. In some ways, adolescence is a period of relatively good health. Many of the health risks of infancy and childhood, such as common infectious diseases, have receded. Many of the health risks of later adulthood, such as cancers, cardiovascular disease and other 'noncommunicable' diseases, are rare. However, adolescence is also the time when people's behaviours become habitual, including risk behaviours such as poor diet, drug use and physical inactivity, which can have a large impact on health in later adulthood. Adolescence is also a time when identities solidify and a large proportion of mental health disorders first appear. If young people become smokers or drinkers, experience mental ill health or become obese during their adolescence, they are likely to continue to experience these into adulthood in ways that will increase their risk of health problems and premature death. Unfortunately, the current generation of young people is, in some ways, less healthy than previous generations. This is likely to have serious consequences for their adult health, quality of life and life expectancy.

Mental health

Let's consider mental health first. Adolescence is a critical period for the onset of mental health problems. Around two thirds of all mental health disorders manifest by the age of 25.[42] The current era is often regarded as a time of crisis for mental health, especially among young people. Globally and in the UK, young people's mental health has significantly worsened since the 1980s,[43,44] particularly among girls.[44,45] This doesn't merely reflect improvements in diagnosing or measuring mental ill health. Nor does it merely reflect a tendency to label as mental illness what might once have been regarded as everyday life problems, such as sadness or worry. The data on trends comes from studies that have used the same standardised, valid ways of measuring mental health to assess year-on-year trends, so the trends identified are likely to be real.

There have been some declines in mental health among adults, but the declines among adolescents have been much more dramatic.[44,46] Broadly speaking, adolescent mental health got worse from the 1980s until around 2000, then stabilised until about 2010, then declined again.[44,47] Suicides rates rose from the 1960s, reduced somewhat from the 1990s to the mid to late 2000s, then rose again.[44] The declines in mental health have centred on 'internalising' problems (such as depression and anxiety) much more than 'externalising' problems (such as misbehaviour and aggression).[48] We don't know for sure the reasons for these trends. Those which date from the 1980s might reflect societies becoming less collective and more individualistic. Some of the more recent downward trends might reflect the impact of family experiences of economic adversity or the rise of social media use by the young. Longitudinal studies tracking young people over time to examine associations between adolescents' use of social media and their later mental health report mixed results, often finding no or small associations.[49,50] It might be that the influence of social media is weaker than commonly imagined. However, it is more likely that social media has harmful effects but that this depends on which specific apps and sites are used and how these are used. It is unlikely that social media explains all the declines in mental health, because these began well before its invention.[44]

In terms of patterns in mental health linked to age, some studies suggest that mental health seems to become worse as people move through secondary school.[51,52] Other studies suggest a U-shaped curve as students move through secondary school, with mental health initially declining then improving slightly nearer the end of secondary school.[53] As well as mental health getting worse overall, it has also become more unequally distributed between different groups of young people. In the UK, socioeconomic inequalities in mental health, where young people from poorer backgrounds experience worse mental health than adolescents from better-off backgrounds, have grown during the last few decades.[54] In the UK, there are also marked inequalities between ethnic groups. These patterns are complex. For example, young people from African communities have better mental health than their White contemporaries, while young people from African Caribbean communities experience worse mental health.[55]

These trends and patterns are of concern. Poor mental ill health in adolescence is likely to carry over into poor mental ill health in adulthood[56] as well as causing immediate harms. For example, depressed or anxious students are more likely to be absent from school or stop attending altogether,[57,58] and adolescents with poor mental health or wellbeing are less likely to do well in academic exams.[59–61]

Violence and substance use

Let's move on to consider various health-related risk behaviours. Despite some declines, risk behaviours such as violence and using various legal and illegal substances remain common among young people. These damage long-term physical and mental health. In most high-income countries, violence and antisocial behaviour, both among adolescents and in society more generally, tended to increase from the 1960s to the 1990s[44] and then tended to fall, in most regions, more recently.[47] The form of violence most associated with childhood and adolescence is bullying. This refers to physical or emotional abuse that is repeated and involves disparities in power. Bullying has declined in many but not all countries.[62] In the UK, rates do not appear to have reduced in recent years and are higher than in many other high-income countries.[30,63] Bullying is most prevalent in the early years of secondary school.[64] Bullying based on ethnicity, disability and sexual orientation is common.[30] Cyberbullying has become more common with the increasing centrality of social media in young people's lives, and this can occur separately from or together with in-person bullying.[47] In England, cyberbullying is particularly common among girls and peaks at age 13 years.[30] Those who are bullied are at greater risk of lower educational attainment and worse mental and physical health during adulthood.[65] Dating and relationship violence and sexual abuse are also common in adolescence, with prevalence varying markedly across different countries and different studies.[66] Psychological abuse is the most common form of dating violence followed by physical and then sexual abuse.[67] Rates of forced sex are stable among girls and falling among boys, but increase with age.[68]

Turning now to 'substance use', this is the umbrella term used to refer to the use of products or substances containing alcohol, nicotine, cannabis or other drugs. In recent decades, there have been big declines in smoking tobacco among young people, as well as less steep declines in their consumption of alcohol and other drugs.[30,69–72] The steepness of the declines varies across countries.[69] There is some evidence in high-income countries that these declines in substance use are now levelling off or, in some cases, even reversing.[73]

While the long-term trend in young people's alcohol consumption is downwards, there is evidence across several countries (including England) since 2018 of an upturn in drinking alcohol and drunkenness among 15-year-old girls. However, during the same period, there were continued decreases in these behaviours among 15-year-old boys.[72] Furthermore, the long-term declines in alcohol use have been greater for boys than girls, and as a result drinking alcohol is now equally common among girls and boys.[70] The declines in drinking alcohol have also been smaller among the most disadvantaged young people and for the heaviest levels of consumption,[70,74] exacerbating health inequalities.

A broadly similar pattern of greater decline for boys than girls emerges for smoking tobacco, and girls are now more likely to smoke than boys.[71] While smoking tobacco has become less common among adolescents, vaping has become more and more common, again particularly among girls.[71] Around one in five girls aged 11–15 years in England now report vaping.[71] Among 15-year-olds in England, 40 per cent of girls and 26 per cent of boys report ever having vaped. The equivalent figures for Wales are 37 per cent and 30 per cent and for Scotland, 40 per cent and 33 per cent. Vaping has been a topic of great controversy among public health planners and researchers, with some seeing this primarily positively as a route out of smoking for adults and others seeing it primarily negatively as a route into smoking for adolescents.[75] Research suggests that vaping can be a gateway to tobacco use for some young people.[76] However, research also suggests that the significant rise in vaping among adolescents has actually been accompanied by a general decrease in the overall acceptability of, and experimentation with, smoking tobacco among young people.[77]

For drug use, trends vary across countries and for different drugs. In the UK, there has been a consistent downward trend. One representative study of 11- to 15-year-olds found that in 2021, 18 per cent reported that they had ever taken drugs, down from 24 per cent in 2018 and with evidence of a long-term decline since 2001.[78] In a study in England, about a fifth (21 per cent) of 15-year-olds said that they had ever tried cannabis, a substantial decrease from 41 per cent in 2002.[30]

Sexual health

Sexual health is an important area for young people in terms of both their immediate but also their future wellbeing. Globally, the picture is complex, with broadly positive trends. Compared to the mid 1990s, adolescent girls are now likely to marry later, delay their first sexual experience, use contraception and delay the birth of their first child.[79] However, in the UK, despite a 70 per cent reduction in under-18 conceptions since 2000, the rate of teenage births remains the highest in western Europe and teenagers are the age group at highest risk of unplanned pregnancy.[80] Age of sexual debut has been decreasing since around the mid-20th century.[81] Most young people do not report 'competent' first sex, defined as using contraception, making an autonomous decision, judging the timing to be right and each partner being equally willing.[82] A lack of competence at first sex is associated with adverse sexual health outcomes.[82]

Sexual harassment is also common in UK secondary schools, with physical harassment being experienced by around three fifths of girls and up to a quarter of boys, and verbal harassment by up to four fifths of girls and half of boys.[83–86] International studies report similar findings.[87–91] Sexual harassment appears to cause significant educational and health harms. Students in US high schools experiencing sexual harassment report finding it hard to pay attention in school, talking less in class, changing their seat in class to get farther away from abusers and (especially among girls) not wanting to go to school.[89,92] Experiencing sexual harassment in adolescence is associated with reduced wellbeing and subsequent victimisation in adulthood.[93,94]

Diet and exercise

Poor diet and lack of physical activity are also important risk behaviours in that they predispose young people to obesity and poorer health in adulthood. Poor diet and obesity are highly, and increasingly, common among young people in most countries.[95] In England, more and more children and adolescents are obese or overweight,[96] and obesity is more common in certain regions and among low socioeconomic groups, girls and some ethnic groups.[96] The trends for physical activity are complex. Among boys but not girls, there has been an overall recent trend towards more physical activity, but with trends varying widely between countries,[97] with UK adolescents remaining highly inactive.

Summary of trends

In summary, then, the current generation of young people is likely to be less mentally healthy, less physically active and more overweight, and there are some concerning recent trends for substance use and sexual risk behaviour. There is also evidence of increasing inequalities across a range of outcomes. Schools are not the only cause of these problems. Poverty, fragmented and fragile communities and families, discrimination, climate change and the lack of regulation of the food, alcohol and tech sectors[98] are very, very important. However, the rest of this chapter examines the evidence that schools are likely to be a significant influence on children and young people's health through the three toxic mechanisms discussed in the previous chapter.

Quantitative evidence for school impacts on health
Differences between individuals

One way that researchers can examine how school experiences might affect students' health is by surveying students on their experiences of school and also on their risk behaviours or health outcomes and then looking for statistical correlations between these at the level of the individual student. It was while doing an analysis of this sort that my interest in school effects on health first developed. Together with colleagues, I was analysing data collected from questionnaire surveys of young people as they progressed through secondary school. Our focus was on which measures of social disadvantage assessed at baseline when students were aged 13–14 years were most likely to be associated with increased risk of teenage pregnancy when students were aged 15–16 years. Although we knew that teenage pregnancy is not a negative experience for all teenagers, we also knew that having a baby while still a teenager tends to be associated with worse health and worse poverty for both the mother and the child. This remains true even after accounting for the fact that teenage parents are generally worse off than other parents to start with.[99–102] We were interested in the association of teenage pregnancy with measures of social disadvantage, such as parental worklessness or living in social or rented housing. While examining these factors, we found to our surprise that the strongest predictor of teenage pregnancy was when a girl reported at baseline that she disliked school.[103] This sparked my interest in how school experiences might be toxic in their effects on health and wellbeing for many students.

There is now quite a lot of quantitative evidence on this question that sheds at least some light on the toxic mechanisms. For example, in terms of the first toxic mechanism of disengagement, there is evidence that students who feel disengaged from school report earlier sexual initiation,[104] more psychological distress[105] and more smoking.[106] In terms of the second toxic mechanism of feeling lack of belonging, there is evidence that mental health, wellbeing, physical activity and sexual health are better and substance use and violence lower among students who report school connectedness or belonging,[105,107–116] good relationships with teachers,[104,106,109,117] involvement in decision-making;[117] happiness with school[109] and quality relationships with peers.[109] In terms of the third toxic mechanism of fear and anxiety, there is evidence that mental health, wellbeing and life satisfaction are better and substance use lower among students who report feeling safe at school,[109,112] having lower school stress or worry[105,109,118] and being in schools that have clear and consistent rules.[119]

This evidence is descriptively important in showing how certain groups of young people experience schools and experience different health outcomes. It points to which subgroups of students need most help. It also supports the possibility that toxic school experiences might cause students to engage in risk behaviours and experience adverse health outcomes. However, it doesn't provide cast-iron evidence for this. Some of the studies cited earlier were cross-sectional; in other words, the student reported their negative experiences of school at the same point in time as they reported engagement in risk behaviours or experience of adverse health outcomes. In such cases, it might be that the health outcome or risk behaviour (such as poor mental health or engagement in violence) is actually the cause, not the consequence, of the negative experience of school. And even the studies that use longitudinal methods to establish that the negative school experience precedes the risk behaviour or health outcome might provide misleading evidence on causality. It is possible that the associations simply reflect the fact that the kinds of student who report negatively about school might also be the kinds of student who report more risk behaviours and poor health outcomes. It might be that rather than schools causing the problem, something else is the real cause, perhaps to do with the families in which students are raised in or the neighbourhoods where they grow up. So we might need to look at other kinds of statistical evidence.

Parallel trends in education and health

We might look to see if trends in poorer educational experiences seem to track trends in risk behaviours or health outcomes. There is quantitative evidence that engagement and belonging have declined and school anxiety has increased, particularly in the UK.[105,107,118,120] Across high-income countries, including England, between 2002 and 2018, there is evidence for an increase in students reporting schoolwork pressure.[121] It might be that these trends in educational experiences explain the trend towards worse mental health among young people in the last few decades. These trends in educational experiences might also explain the trend towards worse diet and less physical activity.

There is also evidence that school disengagement, lack of belonging and worry about schoolwork all get worse during secondary school[30,64,115] (which mirrors the trend towards worse mental health over the course of secondary school that is found in at least some studies). However, as with the studies comparing students, this evidence is far from being solid proof of school effects. It might be that the similarities in trends for educational and health measures are just coincidences and do not indicate that the former causes the latter. But there is more persuasive evidence out there.

Differences between schools

There is evidence that some schools have higher rates of risk behaviours or worse health outcomes than others, even after statistical adjustment for differences in the kinds of students who go to these schools. A large number of research studies across different countries have found that this tendency to 'variance' in behaviours and outcomes between schools is quite large for risk behaviours (such as drinking alcohol, smoking tobacco, using drugs and engaging in violence).[122–127] The variance in mental health between schools seems to be less, though it is still significant.[112,128–130] Research suggests that more of the variance in mental health occurs between individuals rather than between schools.[109,131,132] In the case of diet, there is even less evidence of variance between schools after accounting for the kinds of students who attend them.[106]

It might be that diet is largely explained by family factors and that mental health is more affected by biological, family or early life experiences, whereas risk behaviours are more affected by the school-based mechanisms described in the previous chapter.[122] But another possibility is that the kinds of school mechanism that harm young people's mental health or worsen their diets operate pretty much the same across all or most schools. There is a potential parallel here with physical activity at school, which also does not vary very much between schools. This is not because schools don't affect physical activity at school (they obviously do – for example, through physical education lessons), but because schools all affect it more or less to the same extent.[133] Or it might be that there are school differences in mental health but these only affect the most vulnerable students. There is some evidence that this is the case – for example, for the most socially isolated students.[134] But it is also important to appreciate that even if only a relatively small amount of the overall variance in a risk behaviour or health outcome occurs between schools as opposed to between individuals, this is still likely to be important for overall population health. If this variance reflects the causal influence of schools and if this can be modified by delivering an intervention, then doing so could still be extremely effective in terms of overall population benefit. This is because almost everyone attends school, so small individual changes produce large population changes.[106]

School-level correlates

Not only is there evidence that risk behaviours and health outcomes vary across schools, but specific school-level factors seem to account for these differences. Some studies look at the correlations between particular school-level factors and certain risk behaviours or health outcomes. They adjust statistically for the confounding effects of other factors to try to isolate the causal 'signal' from the 'noise' of other effects. Some studies rely on cross-sectional data where the potential cause is measured at the same time as the potential effect. Others use a longitudinal research design, where the possible cause is measured at an earlier time point than the possible effect so that there is a stronger possibility that correlation points to causation.

Evidence for the disengagement mechanism

In terms of the mechanism of educational disengagement, several studies are notable. There are a raft of studies, some cross-sectional and some longitudinal, reporting that schools that achieve lower rates of student attainment than would be predicted based on student characteristics also have worse rates of student violence and student consumption of tobacco, alcohol and other drugs.[135] There is also evidence that a low aggregate level of educational expectation among students in a school is associated with more students being fearful of violence.[124] A US study tracking high school students over time found that lower school-level aggregate student expectation of going to college was associated with earlier initiation of sex among students,[136] which in turn was associated with adverse sexual health.[137] Remember that in all these studies, it is not the student's own attainment or expectation that is associated with the heath outcome, but rather the aggregate level of attainment or expectation among all students in the school. Our own research tracking adolescents moving through English secondary schools between age 11–12 and age 14–15 found that schools with higher aggregate educational commitment among students had fewer students initiating sex.[104] We also found that lower aggregate school-level commitment was associated with: drug use and bullying victimisation among minoritised students; ever having smoked among minoritised students from less affluent families; and alcohol use in the previous week among less affluent students.[138] A cross-sectional study in Belgium found that secondary schools with overloaded teachers had higher rates of smoking among students.[127] A US study found that high schools with lower ratios of teachers to students had higher rates of student victimisation.[139]

Evidence for the lack of belonging mechanism

In terms of the mechanism of lack of school belonging, several findings are notable. Our own research following students through English secondary schools found that schools with lower aggregate student sense of belonging had higher rates of: drug use ever and in the last month; bullying perpetration and victimisation among males; smoking ever or in the previous week, alcohol use in the previous week and drunkenness among affluent students; and binge drinking among students living with two parents. Studies of secondary schools in Scotland, the broader UK and the US report that schools with a more negative social climate had students with worse mental health and students engaging in more risk behaviours.[106,124,129,140] A cross-sectional study of secondary schools in Finland found that secondary schools with better relationships between staff and students had lower rates of student risk behaviours, better student wellbeing[121] and students reporting fewer health complaints.[141] A German cross-sectional study of secondary schools found that those with a strong focus on attainment but little focus on sport had lower rates of student physical activity.[142] A study tracking students in US high schools found that in schools rated as a having a poor social climate, students with high self-esteem were more likely to be perpetrators of bullying, whereas in schools with a good social climate, students with higher self-esteem were less likely to be perpetrators.[140] An international cross-sectional study of secondary schools found that those with lower levels of cooperation and higher rates of competition among students had lower levels of student sense of belonging.[108,118]

Evidence for the fear and anxiety mechanism

In terms of the mechanism of fear and anxiety, there is some evidence of school effects. A longitudinal US study and a cross-sectional Belgian study each found that high schools in which students report that the rules are not clear, fair, owned or enforced had higher rates of disorder and substance use.[119,127] Our own study, following students through English secondary schools from age 11–12 to age 14–15, examined the effect of a staff-reported measure of school organisational climate that cut across each of the three mechanisms. It validated and used a new measure assessing whether teachers thought that: authority was shared among staff; there were good relationships between staff and students; there was integration of students' academic education and broader development; and there were good links between schools and their local communities. This measure was associated with reduced levels of binge drinking and drug use among students in the previous week, bullying perpetration among boys, bullying victimisation among boys from less affluent families and drunkenness among those from more affluent families.[138]

Conclusion

The current generation of young people is likely to be less mentally healthy. Patterns of bullying and other forms of violence are complex, but rates remain at concerning levels in the UK. Rates of consumption of alcohol, tobacco and other substances have declined in high-income countries, including the UK, but these declines are now levelling off and in some cases consumption is rising again. Sexual health is improving globally, but young people in the UK continue to report high levels of risk and adverse sexual health outcomes. Young people in high-income countries tend to have poor diets and engage in insufficient physical activity, with increasing rates of obesity.

There is consistent evidence from different kinds of studies that there are school effects on risk behaviours and health. The strongest evidence is provided by studies that examine statistical associations between various school-level characteristics and students' health outcomes or risk behaviours. The best of these studies use longitudinal data tracking students over time to establish that the potential causes precede the potential effects. They also adjust for potential confounders so that the causal signal can be distinguished from the noise of other influences. These studies also provide a strong suggestion that these effects occur through the three toxic mechanisms of disengagement, lack of belonging, and fear and anxiety. These studies suggest that within education systems, some schools do a better job of protecting their students from health harm than others. The next chapter focuses on how the toxic effects of schools on adolescent health might be influenced by government policy.

4

Toxic policy? Education policy and its consequences

Introduction

This chapter traces the history of education policy in the UK before briefly discussing the international context. It then looks at the impact of policy developments, positive and negative.

A short history of UK education policy

Origins

In the UK, schools developed over the course of the late 18th and 19th centuries as a means to provide a basic education for the emerging class of industrial workers and a more advanced education for owners, managers and professionals. Their function was as much about sorting as about educating, and there were huge inequities in provision and participation.[143] It was not until after the Second World War that free primary and secondary education was provided for all. But there continued to be massive inequities in the length and quality of schooling. The postwar system of secondary education was officially 'tripartite', comprising: 'grammar' schools teaching academic subjects; 'technical' or 'central' schools teaching applied skills; and 'secondary modern' schools providing basic secondary education. The technical schools did not take off, leaving a system made up of grammar schools for those who passed the '11+' academic exam and secondary moderns for everyone else. Gradually, this system was eroded with the rise of 'comprehensive' secondary schools, which admitted students regardless of prior attainment. The push for comprehensive schools was driven both by the demands of organised labour for better education and by the demands of the middle classes, fearful that their own children might not get into grammar schools.

Upheavals and new settlements

By the late 1970s, the postwar social democratic political settlement, which included a mixed economy with a strong role for the state and an emphasis on professional autonomy in public services, was beginning to collapse.[144] There was a widespread sense that the UK was falling behind other countries economically. There were concerns, particularly on the political Right, that state institutions were inefficient and not achieving their objectives. There was mounting criticism of 'progressive' educational methods (those that emphasised critical understanding and experiential and group learning), seen as not providing young people with the skills required by society and the economy.[143] In 1976, then Prime Minister James Callaghan added to this debate by delivering a speech at Ruskin College Oxford in which he criticised the educational status quo and called for a reorientation of the system to focus on basic skills, employability, a common curriculum and consistent, inspected standards.[145]

Little happened, however, until 1988, when the Conservative government's Education Reform Act introduced major system reforms. There was a new emphasis on consistent academic standards in schools. The Act introduced a national curriculum, including English, mathematics and science, defining what students should be taught and should have learnt by different ages. Previously, schools could set their own curricula. There was also a new emphasis on school managerial autonomy and parental choice. Most schools remained under local authority control but were given more autonomy, receiving a budget reflecting the size of the student body and gaining more powers to recruit and fire staff, albeit with local authorities remaining the formal employer. Some schools became even more independent of local government by taking 'grant-maintained' status so that they owned their buildings and formally employed their staff. The right of parents to choose which school to send their children was also strengthened.

During the 1990s, the Conservative government turned its attention to teacher and school accountability. The Education (School Teacher Appraisal) Regulations 1991 introduced a national system of teacher performance appraisal involving target setting and lesson observations by school leaders. The Education (Schools) Act 1992 introduced the Office for Standards in Education, Children's Services and Skills (known as Ofsted), which regularly inspects state schools. From 1992, league tables have made public a range of data on school performance, including student academic attainment, intended to both inform parental choice and make schools more accountable.

From 1997, the incoming Labour government introduced further reforms but did not deviate from the previous direction of travel. These reforms included the introduction of 'academies', schools that are completely independent of local government and receive a budget direct from central government. Vocational diplomas were introduced to diversify what 14- to 19-year-olds could learn. These were given equivalent status to general certificates of secondary education (GCSEs), the public academic examination taken at age 16 years.

Devolution

The Labour government also introduced devolution for Scotland, Wales and Northern Ireland, and this led to variations in education policy between the UK nations. The Scotland Act 1998 gave the Scottish Parliament legislative control over schooling. Most state schools continued to be managed by a local education authority. In Scotland, there are no academies and almost no mainstream grant-maintained schools. From 2004, Scotland's Curriculum for Excellence has provided some national guidance on learning but gives more leeway to schools than is the case in England. Education Scotland functions as the national inspectorate of primary and secondary schools.[146] Scotland abolished school league tables in 2003. However, from 2017, data on how well Scottish pupils do in reading, writing, listening, talking and numeracy have been published.

Similarly, education policy has been under the control of the Welsh Assembly Government (now the Welsh Government) since 1999. State schools in Wales continue to be managed by local authorities.[147] The national curriculum implemented in Wales from 2022 gives each school more autonomy than those in England to develop their own curricula, underpinned by basic guidance. Estyn is the Welsh schools inspectorate. League tables were abolished in 2001, but in a bid to raise standards, Wales reintroduced the publication of performance information from 2015, with schools colour-coded green, yellow, amber or red to indicate overall performance.

Education is also devolved to the Northern Ireland Assembly. There is a complex array of state schools in Northern Ireland, some of which are managed by the state Education Authority and some of which are more autonomous. Many schools are religious. There remains a much stronger selective system in Northern Ireland than in other parts of the UK. All schools follow the Northern Ireland Curriculum, which is based on the national curriculum used in England. There is a national Education and Training Inspectorate. Northern Ireland abolished school league tables in 2001.

Recent developments

From 2010, the Conservative and Liberal Democrat coalition government introduced further reforms. The Academies Act 2010 allowed all schools in England to opt to become an academy and led to a huge increase in the proportion of schools opting out of local government control. Many of these now belong to 'multi-academy trusts', which may be a local or national network of schools and in some ways have taken the place of local government in mediating between the Department for Education and each school (albeit with no local democratic control). More than four out of five secondary schools in England are now academies, compared to just over one in ten in 2011.[148]

The Importance of Teaching, a 2010 White Paper, introduced the English Baccalaureate (EBacc). This is a metric rather than an actual qualification. It indicates the proportion of students in a school who have gained GCSE passes in English language and literature, mathematics, the sciences, geography or history, and another language. It was intended to encourage schools to focus on a core of academic subjects until the age of 16 years.[148] This removed the GCSE equivalence of some vocational qualifications, so these could no longer count towards school league tables. There were also changes to the national curriculum, resulting in an increase in the volume of content in each subject and a prioritising of teaching factual information.[148] From 2011, 'pupil premium' funding was provided in an effort to boost provision for those students growing up in poverty. Schools receive this funding in line with the number of their students who qualified for free school meals in the previous six years. The Education Endowment Foundation was set up in 2011 to fund research into the effectiveness of pedagogy, focusing in particular on attainment among the most socioeconomically disadvantaged students.[149]

School league tables were amended by the Conservative government in 2016. Previously, the key metric had been the proportion of students getting five GCSEs above a certain grade. This encouraged many schools to 'game' the system by focusing on improving the attainment of a few targeted students at the margins of achieving this minimum threshold (known as 'key marginals'). This had inadvertently led to the relative neglect of, and worse attainment among, lower achievers.[150] There are now six key performance measures for secondary schools: the proportion of students entered for EBacc subjects; the absolute attainment of students in EBacc subjects; 'Progress 8', indicating the progress students make from the end of primary school to the end of Year 11, at age 16 years; 'Attainment 8', which indicates students' absolute attainment in their qualifications at age 16 years (and informs the Progress 8 calculation); the proportion of students achieving grade 5 or above in English and mathematics GCSEs; and pupil destinations – the proportion of students continuing in education, employment or training after Year 11.[148] These metrics are a mix of attainment, threshold and progress measures. Ofsted inspections were also modified so that if a community school (that is, a local authority maintained school) receives an 'inadequate' judgement, it must become an academy. If it is already an academy, then it can be compelled to join a different multi-academy trust. These changes can also occur if a school receives two or more consecutive 'requires improvement' judgements.[148]

International context

Broadly similar policy developments oriented towards boosting school managerial autonomy, national academic standards and curricula, inspections and league tables have occurred in many other countries, including the US.

In the US, federal legislation in the form of the No Child Left Behind (NCLB) Act was introduced in 2002.[151] To receive federal school funding, US states were required to subject students to standardised tests in certain grades. Underperforming schools were publicly named and shamed and made to enact ameliorative actions and allow students to transfer to other schools. NCLB was replaced in 2015 by Every Student Succeeds, which continued the requirement for regular assessments but gives more autonomy to US states in setting standards and determining consequences for underperforming schools.

The impact of policy developments

These developments appear to have had a mixture of positive and negative consequences. Studies suggest that UK schools are now well managed with strong accountability.[152] Evidence suggests that the introduction of league tables in England has led to better attainment.[153] The original threshold metric led to better overall attainment but worse performance among lower attainers as schools focused on key marginal students.[150] However, there is evidence that the introduction in 2016 of a progress measure instead of a threshold measure as a key performance metric produced the intended effect of stopping schools from focusing inappropriately on those students on the margins of achieving five good GCSEs.[154] Research from the US has examined the impact of the NCLB system by comparing states introducing accountability mechanisms with those that had done this at some time previously and so could act as steady state controls. This found significant improvements in academic attainment, equivalent to a 0.15 standard deviation gain on mathematics attainment in fourth grade.[155] Similarly, studies in other countries suggest that increasing school autonomy, at least in high-income countries and in a context of strong school accountability mechanisms, leads to increased attainment.[156–158]

According to the Organisation for Economic Co-operation and Development (OECD), the UK spends above the average on education and spends more per student than in Finland and Japan.[159] Spending is progressive in that schools with disadvantaged intakes receive more funding per student than those with more advantaged intakes.[160] According to international assessments, England has an education system that is both relatively high attaining and relatively equitable in terms of there being a smaller-than-average association between attainment and socioeconomic status, ethnicity and gender.[161] The UK performs better than Finland and Australia for reading and mathematics, but slightly worse for science. The English system achieves better academic results than the Northern Irish, Scottish and Welsh systems.[161,162] England has a stronger focus on a national curriculum, league tables and school autonomy. In Wales, the abolition of league tables in 2001 led to substantially worse attainment.[163] The impact was equivalent to 3.4 per cent fewer students per school achieving at least five good GCSE exam passes. Inequity by socioeconomic status is slightly lower in England than in Scotland and Northern Ireland and only marginally higher than in Wales.[161,164]

However, there remain significant socioeconomic and ethnic inequalities, and these have worsened in the last decade.[164] Of students eligible for free school meals (a measure of family poverty), only 41 per cent were awarded a grade 4 or above in English and maths GCSEs. Among students not eligible for free school meals, the rate was 69 per cent.[164] Although spending is high compared to many comparable countries, it has reduced in real terms since 2010 and since 2013 has been become less progressive with the freezing of the level of the pupil premium payment and with fewer families now qualifying for free school meals because of less generous benefits entitlements.[160,164]

These changes to school systems have been labelled by some as marketisation or neoliberalism,[12,143] but they aren't in reality. Marketisation implies buying and selling. Neoliberalism implies the retreat of the state from the provision of services and the introduction of market mechanisms with as little regulation as possible. The state school system in the UK does not involve buying and selling. Schools remain statutory bodies delivering free public services funded by taxation. They are not permitted to make profits. Parents have some choice about where to send their children, but there is no use of vouchers and no commercial providers in the state system. There has been an increase, not a decrease, in the regulation of state schooling over the last four decades. If headteachers are fired or if schools close, this is almost always due to poor inspection reports or decline in academic performance rather than because school incomes decline as a result of 'consumers' going elsewhere. The system is better described as involving a mix of command and control as well as accountability and transparency.[165] The system is more transparent because of the increased availability of data to citizens. But it is less subject to local democratic accountability because of the transfer of responsibility for schools from local authorities with elected representatives to multi-academy trusts, which are accountable to central government but not local voters.

It is important to remember that the era before these changes was not a progressive paradise. Practice was left to professional judgement. In the best schools and classrooms, this could be amazing, but in the worst, this could be terrible. My experience of school was of some teachers being inspiring but many teachers using incredibly poor pedagogy, not teaching the curriculum or not even being in the classroom. I remember particularly dire music lessons in which, lesson after lesson, we were asked to copy out the lyrics of current pop music songs while the lazy and occasionally violent teacher drank coffee in the staff room.

Toxic impacts of policy developments

Despite some of the consequences of developments in education policy being positive, others have had very harmful consequences, feeding into the toxic mechanisms described in Chapter 2.

Policy impacts on disengagement

In terms of the mechanism of disengagement, schools, particularly since 2010, have increasingly come to take a one-size-fits-all approach to academic education in which every student is expected to excel in exactly the same way. The focus on all students achieving the same academic qualifications partly reflects a concern with equality of opportunity and social mobility. But it also reflects the increasing rigidity of the national curriculum and a desire to keep accountability systems simple and not open to gaming. The result is that schools are encouraged to impose a single standard on all students regardless of the students' aptitudes, preferences, interests or ambitions. Students who are more oriented towards vocational rather than academic learning are particularly poorly served. As one critic has argued:

> The failure of the post-war tripartite system has left vocational courses in a strange limbo-land: vocational courses can provide good routes into employment, yet there is no place for most of them in the accountability framework for schools. ... [S]chools cannot afford to sacrifice subjects which count towards performance measures for qualifications which have GCSE equivalence. (p 103)[143]

Vocational skills received more emphasis during the 1997–2010 Labour government but were marginalised under the subsequent coalition and Conservative governments. There has been a steep decline in students studying technical and vocational subjects.[148]

These problems have been compounded by modern schools increasingly turning towards whole-class teaching, with an emphasis on instruction rather than group work or practical activities.[118,148] This is not explicitly required by government policy, but it may be a natural response to the metrics that schools are judged against as well as the increased level of curriculum content and the renewed emphasis on the learning of facts in the curriculum for most subjects.[148] If so, this is highly counterproductive, as rigorous research studies, including studies funded by the Educational Endowment Foundation, have consistently demonstrated that traditional instruction-based teaching is much less effective than more collective and active approaches to learning.[149] These developments leave many students feeling that schools do not provide them with the pro-school markers of identity, status and transition to adulthood.

Policy impacts on sense of school belonging

In terms of the mechanism of lack of school belonging, modern schools often fail to promote a sense of belonging in a real community. As a result of the increased attention to achieving performance metrics, many schools have come to take a very individualistic view of education. Many schools have become a setting for individual students to be taught, monitored and examined. There has been a downgrading of the sorts of communal activities (such as sports, the arts and pastoral activities) that can help to foster a sense of collective identity, achievement and community. This is partly a consequence of a lack of support from government of school sports and arts, partly a consequence of reduced funding and partly a consequence of giving overwhelming priority to academic attainment in school metrics. Many schools have in effect become merely bundles of individualistic pedagogic and monitoring activities rather than pastoral communities. The lack of school community and belonging can harm mental health and can mean many students lack adequate participation in healthy behaviours, such as sport and real friendships.

Policy impacts on fear and anxiety

In terms of the mechanism of fear and anxiety, modern schools also increasingly use behaviour management approaches emphasising zero tolerance for minor misbehaviour and use of internal exclusion from lessons. Previous studies have explored the harms for young people's mental health that such practices can generate.[166] Our own qualitative research in Park Grove school identified numerous such examples. The school used various technologies and practices to monitor, categorise and punish disruptive students. For example, in staff meetings, senior leaders asked staff to monitor and record information about students' behaviour throughout the day. The students noticed this, referring to the school as a 'prison', lacking private space and with highly restrictive rules. As two students described:

> There is a camera in every hallway you go in. It's like a prison. I've got two dinner ladies every break and lunchtime that are always following me. I ain't even joking! (p 577)[11]

> There are cameras everywhere and teachers patrolling everywhere …. It's too much, you can hardly do nothing if you're me, you're being watched all the time and you're being followed, [they should] leave me in peace! (p 557)[11]

The students were frequently made to be isolated from other students all day within what was referred to in somewhat Orwellian language as 'inclusion centres'. Such methods are, however, less effective than other methods of preventing violence and protecting students from harm.[167] Students and staff report that English schools are often disorderly with lots of time spent off task.[64] And contemporary schools often ramp up the pressure on students to maximise attainment while failing to support them. These developments contribute to many students feeling unsafe and anxious at school.

Overall trends

Overall, there is certainly evidence that increased autonomy and accountability, as well as improved management, can lead to improved attainment.[152,155,157,158,168,169] Nonetheless, globally and in the UK, the long-term trend has actually been a decline in academic attainment.[170] This has been accompanied, as we saw in Chapter 3, by a significant worsening of mental health and some aspects of physical health. Though not definitive, there is some evidence for a possible trade-off in national school systems between promoting attainment and promoting quality of life or wellbeing.[107,162,171] England does relatively well in terms of attainment but relatively badly in terms of wellbeing.[170] Furthermore, despite evidence of the English schooling system performing relatively well in international assessments, young adults in England actually do worse than those in other countries and worse than older English cohorts in terms of employability skills.[164] Something is clearly wrong.

Conclusion

Education policy has pivoted in the last four decades to emphasise school autonomy and accountability. There is evidence that these developments have brought some benefits in terms of school management efficiency, consistency of standards and student attainment. However, it is also likely that some aspects of these changes have contributed to the toxic mechanisms of educational disengagement, lack of school belonging, and fear and anxiety. In particular, there has been a narrowing of the curriculum, a reversion to regressive and ineffective pedagogies, an erosion of collective experiences in schools, a use of cruel and ineffective disciplinary methods and a lack of support for students coping with the pressures of schoolwork. Thus, despite some positive developments, something is wrong with schools and school systems. The rest of this book explores what steps are being taken to improve this situation and which of these are actually effective.

5

Health interventions in schools as sticking plasters

Introduction

Schools are increasingly required to address student health and wellbeing. This development seems to be somewhat in contradiction to the picture presented in the previous chapter of schools having become overwhelmingly focused on maximising individual educational attainment. However, it makes more sense when viewed as the system adapting itself to try to compensate for some of its own adverse consequences.

Types of school health intervention

A variety of health and wellbeing interventions are now delivered in schools. Some of these are 'universal' interventions, aiming to promote the health and wellbeing of all students. These can include health education classes, providing, for example, sex or drugs education.[172,173] They can include social and emotional education lessons focused on learning to manage ones emotions and relationships.[174] And they can include classes and other activities focused on meditation and mindfulness, also to help manage one's emotions and relationships.[175] Relationships, sex and health education is now a statutorily required subject in all English schools.[176]

As well as interventions delivered to all students to promote health and wellbeing, other interventions target students engaged in certain risk behaviours or experiencing certain mental or physical health problems. These include cognitive behavioural therapy[177,178] and counselling for students with anxiety or depression as well as group interventions for students experiencing problems with substance use. In 2017, the government initiated a new programme of mental health services in schools, with a focus on cognitive behaviour therapy to address mild to moderate anxiety and depression, and created school mental health support teams to deliver these.[179] Schools can also refer their students for targeted interventions delivered outside school if students need help with, for example, mental health or substance use.

Evidence of impacts

Some of these interventions, such as social and emotional learning and various school-based mental health services, have been found in rigorous evaluations to effectively promote student health and contribute to improvements in academic attainment.[174,180] For other interventions, it may still be a good idea to deliver them in schools even if their effects are not so dramatic. For example, most people would agree that it is important to provide sex and relationships education in schools – even though research suggests that the effects on health outcomes, such as teenage pregnancy and sexually transmitted infections, are quite limited – because young people have a right to learn about this.[172] Other interventions have been found often to be ineffective. These include school-based mindfulness (largely because students are reluctant to regularly meditate),[175] teachers providing some forms of mental health support to students[181] and some cognitive behavioural therapy approaches to address bullying.[182]

The potential for harm

Some interventions have even been found to be harmful. Interventions that target students who are already involved in risk behaviours, such as drug use, and put them together in group work are particularly prone to inadvertent harmfulness.[183] This can arise because students feel stigmatised, which entrenches rather than reduces their involvement in risk behaviours. It can also arise when group work is poorly facilitated and the groups become places for risk behaviours to be learnt or reinforced (known as 'positive deviancy training') rather than challenged.

An example of a harmful intervention

In the first decade of the new millennium, with Meg Wiggins and other colleagues, I evaluated a government programme called the Young People's Development Programme. This involved local youth work clubs recruiting students from different local schools who were deemed by their teachers or other professionals as being at risk of truancy, substance use or teenage pregnancy. The work, which was intended to be provided after school, involved sports, arts, health education and mentoring.[184] A similar earlier intervention delivered in New York City had brought about significant reductions in teenage pregnancy rates.[185] We evaluated the programme using what is known as a quasi-experimental design. We compared the group of young people who were participating in the programme with a group of similar young people participating in youth clubs in areas not in receipt of the programme. These areas were matched with programme sites in terms of: region; local deprivation; rates of teenage pregnancy; whether they were in rural, urban or seaside locations; and the types of organisation providing the local youth work. Within these comparison areas, we recruited participants who were similar to the programme participants by asking local workers to identify young people they deemed at risk of school exclusion, substance use or teenage pregnancy. We surveyed the young people in both groups at baseline and then 9 and 18 months later.

Among the civil servants who had led the development of the programme, the charity that was coordinating the programme and the local youth clubs that were delivering the programme, there were high hopes that a positive impact could be achieved in England, similar to New York City. However, from early on in the programme, things seemed to be going wrong. Local sites struggled to recruit enough participants. Then an analysis of initial impacts after nine months indicated that more young people in the intervention than the comparison group were reporting truanting from school. We presented these results to the civil servants. They suggested that maybe we could just drop that measure. We gulped and insisted that it had to remain if the research were to have any integrity. When we completed our study, we found to our horror that at final follow-up, 18 months after baseline, young women in the intervention group reported much higher rates not only of truancy but also of temporary exclusions from school, sexual activity and pregnancy. Young women receiving the programme were between 2.5 and 3 times more likely than those in the comparison group to become pregnant.

Our evaluation used quasi-experimental rather than experimental methods. An experimental design would have randomised young people or local areas to get or not get the intervention. This would have allowed for the fairest comparison. Instead, the areas to receive the programme had already been decided. We were not able to get local youth clubs to use randomisation to decide which young people did or didn't get entry to their local programme. So the next best thing was to use a quasi-experimental design, assembling our comparison group using the methods of matching described earlier. Quasi-experimental designs are more likely than experimental designs to be subject to confounding. This simply means that baseline differences between groups make for a less fair comparison.

Because of this, the civil servants were sceptical about our results and reluctant to abandon their programme on the basis of these. They provided more funding for us to subject our data to other analyses to check if the results might instead be explained by confounding or by other factors. We carried out further adjustments. We undertook analyses that took account of the propensity of different types of young people to join our programme and comparison groups. We weighted the data to check that different drop-out rates in each arm were not to blame for the effects. Rather than leading to a reduction in the apparently harmful impact of the programme, these analyses actually suggested the real effect was even larger. Because of this and because of the sheer size of the difference in pregnancy rates between our two groups, we concluded that the Young People's Development Programme was indeed harmful. The programme was shut down.

This harmful effect was probably due to both the mechanisms of stigmatisation and positive deviancy training, described earlier. Unlike in the US, the intervention intentionally set out to recruit specific students deemed by their schools as being at particular risk. In contrast, the original US intervention had focused on all the young people in poor neighbourhoods. The English programme was also often in practice used as an alternative, rather than an extracurricular complement, to normal school. This adaptation was not intended by those leading the programme and occurred because local youth work clubs were struggling to achieve strict recruitment targets on which their funding depended. Their solution was to offer the programme during normal school hours as an alternative to school. Many schools jumped at the chance to offload their most disengaged and disruptive students. As a result of these intended and unintended adaptations, participating student may have felt stigmatised, further eroding their engagement with school. This may have increased their involvement with risk behaviours, such as early sexual activity, as an alternative marker of identity, status and transition to adulthood. Bringing together the most at-risk young people from across a local area, many of whom may not have known each other previously, and involving them in loosely structured youth club activities may have led to positive deviancy training on steroids.

I was interviewed about our evaluation by John Humphrys on BBC Radio 4's *Today* news programme. The famously combative Humphrys snorted when I described the results and asked whether the young people were simply having sex with each other at the youth clubs. Probably not. But it was highly possible that the clubs were sites where young people having attitudes supportive of early and risky sexual activity was normalised and reinforced. This programme shows that it cannot be assumed that well-meaning interventions will always bring benefits. We know that pharmaceutical and surgical interventions can cause harms. It is also the case that social interventions, including those aiming to improve the health and wellbeing of school students, can sometimes cause more harm than good.[183,186]

Are mental health interventions inflating the prevalence of mental ill health?

There has been a suggestion recently that there might be a similar problem concerning school mental health interventions.[187] The suggestion is that interventions that raise awareness of mental health problems, particularly among adolescents, cause 'prevalence inflation'. This might happen by encouraging young people to over-interpret everyday concerns as mental health symptoms. This might lead to worsened mental health – for example, because these young people then avoid stressful situations, which only reinforces their anxiety.[187] Evidence in support of this hypothesis includes findings from a meta-analysis that school-based cognitive behavioural therapy can lead to more internalising symptoms, such as anxiety and depression.[188,189] Other evidence in support of this theory comes from a trial of a mindfulness intervention in English secondary schools that found this led to more depressive symptoms and worse mental wellbeing among students with baseline increased risk.[175]

However, I would say that, overall, the evidence for this particular hypothesis is pretty weak. The analysis of studies of school cognitive behavioural therapy actually comes from a review of school-based anti-bullying interventions, a subgroup analysis of which found that cognitive behavioural therapy led to more internalising symptoms.[188] More comprehensive reviews of school-based cognitive behavioural therapy suggest that, in fact, this provides small beneficial effects for students with and without baseline symptoms.[190,191] The trial of school-based mindfulness did indeed find short-term harmful effects among the subgroup of students with baseline increased risk of mental health problems. However, this effect dissipated according to longer-term follow-up at 18 months.[189] Overall, the trial found no effects, and this is consistent with evidence that the intervention prompted very few students to practise mindfulness.[175] It's unlikely that an intervention that was practised so little would have harmful effects. In light of this, the subgroup effect on depression is most likely a chance false positive finding, which is extremely common when there are multiple tests of effect among different subgroups. Even if it is real, the finding of harm among those who already had depressive symptoms at baseline does not actually fit with the prevalence inflation hypothesis, which is about harm among the previously well.

Problems with delivery

But my disputing of the prevalence inflation hypothesis does not mean that I am wholly in favour of the proliferation of school-based interventions to address mental or physical health. Even when such interventions are effective in promoting students' health (which, as we have seen, is often not the case), schools may really struggle to deliver these at scale. During the previous Labour government, there was an attempt to implement a national programme of social and emotional aspects of learning. While there is good evidence that social and emotional learning can improve mental health and academic attainment,[174,180] the national programme was found, in a rigorous evaluation, not to have benefited students. This was attributed to variable, and often quite poor, implementation by schools.[192] Many studies have established that fidelity of implementation is critically important for social interventions to be effective.[193] Overburdened schools whose main focus is academic attainment are unlikely to have the time, the right staff or enough resources to implement many health interventions with fidelity.[182]

There is little space in school timetables and certainly not enough space for a curriculum for every health or wellbeing outcome. My team and I have conducted countless studies of classroom education on topics such as bullying, drugs and sex education. School staff very often cite the lack of timetable space as a key factor in poor delivery of health education.[167,173,194] Staff expertise can also hinder good implementation. Teachers are not therapists, and it is hard to train them to become therapists because of the different capacities and skill sets required.[182] There is some evidence that targeted mental health interventions are more effective in schools when delivered by specialist staff rather than teachers.[191] Teachers may even struggle with teaching health education in the classroom, because this requires different sorts of skills to those needed for teaching academic lessons. For example, there is evidence that teachers struggle to manage the detailed health information, more discursive style and sensitive subject matter in sex education lessons.[195] So teachers may not be the best providers of school-based health interventions. But schools struggle to be able to afford to employ other providers for such work, such as costly clinical professionals or external health educators.

Even if schools do have the time, capacity and resources to deliver health interventions well, they may lack the motivation. School leaders may question whether it is really their role to deliver additional interventions to promote student health and wellbeing. This is especially so given that education is their core business and they already have very challenging performance targets to meet for educational attainment. In the absence of management support, interventions are unlikely to be delivered well and, therefore, be effective or sustained.[196] There is also the possibility that some school health interventions will be unacceptable to students, as appeared to be the case with the trial of mindfulness in schools[197] and might also sometimes be the case for some students for some forms of sex education.[195]

Sticking plasters, not solutions

Even where they are effective and even if they could be delivered at scale, these interventions are essentially sticking plasters. They aim to compensate for rather than disrupt the toxic mechanisms described in this book. They need to be constantly redelivered to cohort after cohort of students. They use up lesson time, teacher training time and school resources, all of which could instead be used for schools' core business. We are not recommending that schools do none of these activities. Some are effective and can benefit students not only in terms of their health but also in terms of their education.[174,198] Some health education can even be integrated into academic learning to deliver a double dividend. For example, in the UK, the Ariel Trust's Plastered and the British Heart Foundation's Money to Burn interventions incorporate into mathematics lessons education about the risks, respectively, of drinking alcohol and smoking tobacco. To inform class discussions about alcohol harms, Plastered gets students to calculate the units of alcohol that are consumed and presents statistical data on attitudes to alcohol. Money to Burn gets students to calculate how much smokers spend on cigarettes. We conducted a review of all the evidence on interventions that integrate health education into academic lessons and found that such interventions could reduce rates of smoking, drinking and drug use among students.[199] But overall I think that there needs to be less emphasis on interventions to compensate for toxic school mechanisms and more emphasis on interventions to disrupt these mechanisms.

Conclusion

This chapter described the rise of health interventions delivered in schools or outside of school for school students. It has shown how these can be of variable effectiveness, with some being very effective but many others being ineffective or even harmful. It described our evaluation of the Young People's Development Programme, an intervention that was found to be harmful. Even when school-based health interventions are effective, schools may lack the motivation, time, capacity or resources to deliver interventions with the fidelity needed to ensure they are effective. While there is a role for some school health interventions, they are not a panacea and do not remove but merely compensate for the toxic mechanisms of school disengagement, lack of school belonging, and fear and anxiety, which can harm young people's health. On their own, these sorts of ameliorative interventions are not going to detoxify schools. However, there is another way, as discussed in the next chapter.

6

The Learning Together intervention: effective school detox in England

Introduction

This chapter first describes the limitations of observational studies. Then it covers some theories that can help us understand the impact of schools on young people. The Learning Together intervention is described, and evaluation of programme delivery and impacts is discussed.

The limitations of observational studies

Chapter 3 described evidence of statistical associations between, on the one hand, various measures of school-level characteristics and, on the other, various risk behaviours and health outcomes among the students attending these schools. The best of these studies used longitudinal designs tracking students over time so that it was clear that the school-level characteristics in question were present before, and therefore could plausibly be a cause of, the student risk behaviour or health outcome. These studies also tried to adjust statistically for possible 'confounding' factors that could provide alternative explanations for why students in certain schools engaged in more risk behaviours or had worse health outcomes. These confounders might be characteristics of the students who attended the schools, their families or the neighbourhoods where they lived. Such studies provide quite plausible evidence that schools might influence their students' involvement in risk behaviours and health outcomes.

However, these studies are still quite limited in what they can tell us about school effects and the three toxic mechanisms. Some of the studies were cross-sectional, and with these it is hard to know whether the school-level factor in question is the cause or the consequence of the risk behaviour or health outcome. Even the longitudinal studies do not provide watertight evidence of causality. It remains a possibility that unmeasured confounding factors are the real cause, being associated both with the school-level factor suggested as a cause and the risk behaviour or health outcome suggested as a consequence. Consider one of the stronger studies cited in Chapter 3, a US study tracking high school students over time.[136] This found that there was a tendency towards younger age of sexual initiation in schools with lower overall student expectations of going to college. Because the study focused on expectations aggregated at the school level rather than looking at expectations at the student level, it did appear to indicate that there was something about being in certain schools with overall low educational expectations (rather than individual students having lower expectations themselves) that might predispose students to earlier sexual initiation.

Furthermore, this study was longitudinal, so it measured the lower school-level academic expectations before it measured the earlier initiation of sex. It also adjusted for many factors to do with the students and their families to check that it was not actually one or more of these that explained earlier sexual initiation in some schools. These included students' ethnicity, alcohol use, delinquency, physical development and educational attainment as well as family structure, parental education, parental attitude to children's sexual activity and parental monitoring of their children. But there might still have been something about the sorts of students who attended the school and their families that explained both the lower levels of educational expectations and students' early sexual initiation which had nothing to do with the way the schools were run. Possible factors that the study did not adjust for include the socioeconomic status, income or benefits entitlement of students' families. It might be that certain schools were attended by students from families with lower incomes and it is this, rather than anything to do with school organisation, which explained the students tending to have lower educational expectations and starting to have sex younger.

In identifying this limitation, I am not trying to pick on this particular study. Instead, I am highlighting that there will always be limitations in what we can learn about causality from studies that measure different characteristics of schools and their students and then look for associations between these. Furthermore, such studies cannot tell us whether the school-level factors they examine can actually be modified to lower students' involvement in risk behaviours or improve their health. These studies are called 'observational' studies. This chapter and the next present evidence from experimental and quasi-experimental studies, which overcome these problems by examining the effects of interventions that aim to modify the school environment and then assess the subsequent effects of this on student behaviours or health outcomes. Experimental and quasi-experimental studies actually set out to change reality and then examine the consequences of doing this. They are 'interventional' rather than merely observational. As a result, they provide much stronger evidence of causality. They also tell us whether the school characteristics that we are interested in can be modified to lower student risk and improve their health. But before looking at these sorts of studies,

I want to consider some of the theories that have been used to think through how we might modify the school environment to make it more promoting of student health.

Theorising school impacts on risk and health

At worst, theories can feel like unnecessarily abstract and complicated ways to see the world that have little to do with practical actions to help people. But, at best, theories can provide a framework for thinking through how we understand problems and what actions we might take to address them.[200] Various psychological and sociological theories have been used to propose how school environments can be modified to improve students' physical and mental health and their educational attainment.[201] Some of these include mechanisms that look like good ways of disrupting the toxic mechanisms described in this book. They suggest ways that schools can build a sense of educational engagement, sense of belonging, and sense of safety and support among students. As I became interested in developing interventions to change school organisation in order to improve student health, I reviewed the theories out there to try to find ones that could help inform interventions.

The social development model

The social development model is a well-known general psychological theory of learning.[202] It doesn't aim to consider schools in particular, but it has interesting things to say that could have a bearing on schools. It proposes that young people learn both pro- and antisocial behaviours (including health-related risk behaviours) from those around them by observing others who are engaged in certain behaviours, trying out these behaviours themselves, developing skills in and practising these behaviours, and receiving positive or negative feedback when they enact these behaviours. The idea is that positive feedback will reinforce their engagement with the behaviour, while negative feedback will do the opposite.

This model suggests that young people will be more likely to bond to school, develop attachments to pro-social peer groups and develop commitment to pro-school behaviours when schools provide them with positive opportunities to learn, develop skills, practise behaviours and be rewarded for them.[202] Such bonds will tend to reduce young people's association with anti-school peers and risk behaviours. If young people do not bond with school, they will be more likely to become involved in anti-school peer groups and learn antisocial risk behaviours from these peers.

However, because the social development model is a psychological theory, it does not have much to say about institutions. It does not describe the specific features of a school likely to promote bonding. And it only helps us to think about how health risks will arise from antisocial behaviours; it doesn't help us think about how the school environment will affect mental health.

Social capital theory

Social capital theory is another well-known general theory. Because it is a sociological theory, it tells us a little more about how schools as institutions might affect behaviour. Social capital is defined as comprising social networks that enable group or individuals to achieve certain goals.[203] The idea is that we don't just get our power to do what we want from how much money we have or other attributes we possess as individuals, such as communication skills. We also get power from the relationships we are involved in. For example, we might be better able to get a certain job if we know people who already do that sort of job. Some theorists have suggested that social capital is most enabling when social networks are stable, intergenerational and involve norms of reciprocal obligation.[204] Robert Putnam introduced the distinction between 'bonding' social capital (strong ties between similar individuals) and 'bridging' social capital (weaker ties between disparate individuals and groups).[25] Bonding social capital has the potential to lower aspirations by enforcing conformity, while bridging social capital has the potential to raise them by introducing new ideas or attitudes.[203]

These ideas might thus predict that within a school, good bridging social capital between staff and students has the potential to encourage students to develop pro-school behaviours and higher educational expectations and avoid the sorts of anti-school peer groups that might promote risk behaviours, such as substance use and violence. While raising some interesting possibilities about the role of teachers, social capital theory still doesn't tell us very much about what schools need to do specifically to prevent risk behaviours. And it has little to say about mental health.

The theory of human functioning and school organisation

Disappointed by the limited usefulness of these general psychological and sociological theories, I eventually came across the theory of human functioning and school organisation, developed by English health researchers Wolfgang Markham and Paul Aveyard. This is a sociological theory much more specifically focused on schools.[205] It proposes that for young people to be able to make healthy choices and adopt health behaviours, they need both the reasoning abilities to make good choices and the social support to implement these choices.[205] The theory suggests that schools need to ensure students develop these reasoning abilities and social affiliations. For this to happen, students need to engage with a school's 'instructional order' (in other words, teaching and learning). Students also need to develop a sense of belonging within a school's 'regulatory order' (in other words, the school community and its norms). The theory suggests that engagement and belonging are easier for middle-class students because they have been socialised for this to be the 'default setting' and because the school has broadly the same cultural values as the families of these students. But, often, engagement and belonging are likely to be harder to build for disadvantaged students.

Therefore, to engage all students, the school needs to work a little harder. One of the things that schools need to do is erode some of the 'boundaries' that make them feel alienating for some disadvantaged students. Here, I am not talking about boundaries as they are commonly thought of, referring to rules or norms of what is and isn't allowed. The theory of human functioning and school organisation uses the term in another way to refer to social barriers between staff and students, distinctions between different areas of learning and social differences between the school and its local community. Let's consider each of these in turn.

In terms of the boundaries between staff and students, these involve differences in status and culture. Schools need to work to improve these relationships and transform them from being merely instrumental and often oppositional to also being affective and collegial. This does not mean taking away teachers' authority or throwing away school rules. But it does mean teachers and students getting to know each other better as humans rather than just as role holders in the institution. They need to develop empathy for each other.

In terms of the boundaries between academic subjects, to someone who has been through secondary and especially higher education, it might seem perfectly natural to divide up how we learn about the world into separate academic subjects. But this is not natural to a child transitioning from primary into secondary school, especially if the child has grown up in a family where few if any members have had higher or even upper secondary education. Eroding these boundaries does not mean abandoning the teaching of academic subjects. But it does mean explaining and exploring the boundaries of these academic categories. It might mean placing more emphasis on how learning in these subjects might be practically useful. For some students, it might mean teaching the same content but in more interdisciplinary ways – for example, through project-based learning.

In terms of boundaries between the culture of the school and that of the local community, these involve differences in culture or social values. Eroding these does not mean that the role of schools is merely to validate existing values and knowledge in the community, rather than introducing students to other values and knowledge. But it does mean starting from where students are and not dismissing local culture. This is particularly important where the local community includes people from different cultures or people whose cultures are different from those of the school's staff.

As well as eroding these boundaries, the theory of human functioning and school organisation suggests that schools should 'reframe' learning and other provision so that they bend a little more towards students' own needs and priorities. Rather than students being in school to help the school meet its goals, the school should be there to help students achieve their goals. In terms of curriculum, this might mean ensuring that students learn about the things that interest them or which they need to realise their aspirations. This does not mean throwing away the curriculum and focusing on students' interests to the exclusion of all else, but it does mean that the curriculum should be diverse. In terms of pedagogy, it might mean ensuring that lessons involve active ways of learning, where students contribute actively, rather than lessons just using didactic instructional methods. In terms of school organisation, it might mean giving students a say in some of the decisions that affect them. This does not mean surrendering all authority to the students, but it does mean involving students and teaching them how to contribute constructively to decisions and learn how to be good citizens.

Promoting student engagement with the instructional order and a sense of belonging with the regulatory order should enable students to develop the reasoning ability and social relationships required to make healthy decisions and maintain healthy behaviours. Students can learn about health partly by this being integrated into a broader curriculum and partly by developing the general learning skills that will help them learn about health throughout their lives. Students should learn social and emotional skills naturally and actively throughout all aspects of school life, not merely through social and emotional learning classes. Students will derive a sense of identity, status and transition to adulthood through being valued members of the school community who are recognised to make tangible contributions in different areas of school life. They will, therefore, feel less inclined to join anti-school peer groups or engage in risk behaviours as alternative ways of defining their identity, status and transition to adulthood.

The theory of human functioning and school organisation was a revelation to me because it engages with the detail of how schools are organised, because it has something to say about the potential effects of this on risk behaviours and health, and because it so clearly resonates with the toxic mechanisms involving educational disengagement, lack of belonging, and fear and anxiety, which emerged from our qualitative research. Although some of the concepts, such as boundaries and reframing, were complex, it felt clear to me that the theory could be used to inform a practical intervention for schools.

The Learning Together intervention

We drew on some of these ideas to develop and implement Learning Together.[167,206] This intervention aimed to increase student engagement, belonging, and safety and support in English secondary schools and through this to reduce bullying and aggression as the primary intended outcomes. It also aimed, as secondary intended outcomes, to reduce smoking, drinking alcohol and drug use to improve mental health and health-related quality of life and to improve academic attainment. I developed the intervention with my colleagues Russell Viner, Adam Fletcher and Lyndal Bond, who are health researchers, and Miranda Perry, who is a teacher and educational expert.

Activities

The Learning Together intervention involved several activities, described next.

Needs assessment

We did questionnaire surveys with students at the end of their first year of secondary school (Year 7, when students are aged 11–12 years). The questionnaire was completed in private by students, in classrooms. It asked them about their: experiences at school; attitudes to school; engagement with lessons; sense of belonging; relationships with staff and other students; and experiences of bullying and other health-related risk behaviours. We then prepared a short report for each school, summarising the needs and views of the school's students and comparing these to the views of students in other schools delivering Learning Together. The reports focused on the overall picture at school level and did not include the names of students or any information that could identify them.

Action groups

We gave schools a manual to guide the intervention, which directed and supported them to form 'action groups' comprising around six staff and six students. We asked schools to include senior and less senior staff with different roles. We asked that a mixture of students be included to reflect the diversity within the school. We asked schools to involve some of the less engaged and lower-attaining students rather than just the usual 'good' students. We also provided each school with an external facilitator to help ensure that everyone in the action groups could contribute their views and that the groups stayed focused on deciding on and delivering actions. The facilitators had experience working in schools, often as a headteacher or deputy headteacher. The action groups met around six times per year. We asked that schools treated these as 'grown-up' meetings with proper agendas, minutes being taken and tea and biscuits provided.

  Each action group was asked to review the school's report on student needs and decide what actions the school should take in response. For example, in a school where students reported feeling isolated, the school might decide to develop a peer buddying scheme, and in a school where students reported poor relationships with staff, the school might decide to lengthen the registration period so that students could get to know their form tutor better. We hoped not only that the action group would make sensible decisions that would directly benefit students, but also that the very act of having an action group involving students contributing to decisions would achieve a cultural change in the school. We hoped that students and staff in the group would work well together and develop better relationships. We also hoped that the broader group of students not involved in the action group would hear about the work and feel more positively about the school because they knew that it was taking actions to benefit them. The action group was also tasked with overseeing the implementation of restorative practice across the school.

Restorative practice

We have Lyndal Bond to thank for this element. It was her insight that restorative practice was consistent with our aims and would be a useful way for schools to reduce bullying. Restorative practice is a way to deal with conflict, bullying or misbehaviour in schools. The traditional approach schools have tended to take with these issues is punitive: staff judge who is to blame for an incident and punish that person in the hope that this will deter future trouble. Restorative practice takes a different approach. It views conflict, bullying or misbehaviour as a symptom of poor relationships. It aims to restore relationships so that future incidents are avoided. For example, in response to one student having bullied another, the school might facilitate a meeting between the perpetrator and victim. The meeting would explore what happened, with each participant listening to what the other had to say. The victim would, if they felt comfortable, describe the hurt and harm caused. The perpetrator would listen and be encouraged to take responsibility for their actions. The perpetrator might be encouraged to propose steps they should take to redress this harm and avoid future incidents. Restorative practice is a non-punitive approach to addressing conflict, bullying or other misbehaviour, but using it does not mean punitive approaches have to be abandoned. The two approaches can be used alongside one another. It might often still be appropriate for perpetrators to be punished. The punishment can be decided in the light of the extent of the harm caused or the extent to which the perpetrator has taken responsibility for their actions.

Restorative practice requires skilled facilitation by staff if it is to bring benefits and avoid unintended harms. In order to use restorative practice, we trained all staff in each school on the basics of restorative practice, its underlying philosophy and the language used. This training lasted a couple of hours. Our aim was to build support for this approach across all staff and encourage them to use restorative language in preventing conflict, dealing with minor incidents and making referrals for more major incidents. In order to handle more major incidents, we trained four or five staff in each school to be able to lead restorative meetings. This training occurred over three days and went into much more detail about restorative practice. It included discussions and role-play to ensure staff developed the skills needed. This training was developed and delivered by a company accredited for this training – L30 Relational Systems, led by Mark Finnis.

Social and emotional learning

We also provided schools with lesson plans and slides to allow teachers to deliver social and emotional learning lessons to students. We hoped that these lessons would help students manage their emotions and their relationships better. We also hoped that these lessons would enable students to develop the skills needed to contribute towards restorative practice when they encountered it. I have to admit that this was the element of the intervention that we were least interested in as scientists. We knew from previous studies that social and emotional learning lessons could have positive benefits for students,[174,180] as reported in Chapter 5. We were much more interested in seeing whether our more innovative, non-classroom-based elements could bring benefits. But we were encouraged to include the social and emotional learning lessons by the scientific members of the panel that reviewed our proposal on behalf of the funder.

Phasing of activities

Schools delivered this work for three years. The training was all delivered at the start. At this time, schools also received the manual and all the lesson materials. The surveys were repeated each year to furnish action groups with updated reports on student needs. The external facilitator supported action groups for two years and schools were then charged with facilitating their own action groups for the final year.

Theory of change

Learning Together was guided by what is known as a theory of change. The theories described earlier in this chapter (the social development model, social capital theory and the theory of human functioning and school organisation) are theories about how we think the world works. In contrast, theories of change are theories about how we think a particular intervention will achieve its intended outcomes.

Our theory of change for Learning Together was influenced by the theory of human functioning and school organisation. It theorised that the delivery of the different elements would reduce bullying and aggression among students and improve secondary health outcomes for them by modifying boundaries and framing within a school. It theorised that boundaries between students and teachers, and between academic education and broader learning, would be eroded. It theorised that reframing school provision would mean student preferences and needs could be addressed more directly. It theorised that such changes would encourage more students, especially those from disadvantaged backgrounds, to commit to their school's instructional order (learning and teaching) and regulatory order (community and norms). This would help students choose and implement more pro-school and healthy behaviours, avoiding risk behaviours and mental distress. Thus, we hoped to disrupt the toxic mechanisms described in Chapter 2. Our evaluation collected empirical data to find out if the intervention succeeded in doing this.

Evaluation of delivery

Emily Warren and I examined the process of implementation using a 'process evaluation' that employed both quantitative and qualitative research methods. We used quantitative research to identify how well the intervention had been delivered. We asked our trainers and the teachers to log what they had delivered. We observed some training sessions, some action groups and some lessons to assess the accuracy of teachers' self-reports. Because of the sensitive nature of restorative practice meetings, we did not observe those. We also included questions about students' involvement in the intervention in our follow-up questionnaire surveys of students, two and three years into the project. We used qualitative research to develop a deeper, richer understanding of teachers' and students' experiences of and views on Learning Together. We undertook one-to-one interviews as well as focus groups to explore stories about how the intervention was delivered, whether it was acceptable and what impacts it appeared to have. We learnt lots of useful things as a result of the process evaluation.

Poor delivery of social and emotional skills lessons

We found that in terms of delivery, most aspects of the intervention were well delivered but the social and emotional learning lessons were not. Some schools already had social and emotional skills lessons, which they did not want to replace. In other schools, there was no space in school timetables to deliver our lessons. In some schools, the staff were not impressed by our lesson materials and did not use them. Some teachers said that they adapted the materials to make the curriculum more engaging for their pupils.

This was often felt necessary because the lessons were viewed as too simplistic or boring. As one teacher explained: 'Sometimes to make it … I had to make it sometimes a little bit more visual or include videos or try to … sometimes approach it from a different … in a slightly different way'(p 67).[207]

Success with action groups

The action groups, in contrast, were well delivered and well received. Schools were better able to run action groups and deliver the actions these bodies recommended when school senior managers sat on the group or otherwise supported it.[208] Students liked participating in action groups because these felt like real meetings that achieved change, in contrast to school council meetings (the usual forum where schools seek student views, which often do not result in action). As one student commented:

> The topics are good on the action group [compared to the school council]. *We actually talk about things that we do here, what's good for the future, stuff like that*, like I said in the first place about the CCTV [which is] going to be improved and, you know, they listen. (p 328, italics in original)[209]

Staff also felt it was good to involve students in decision-making. This included those students who were not the usual, engaged students, as senior staff explained:

> The action group has been really important. It's the first time in the school, as far as I understand, that you've had students working with staff – *and properly working with staff* […] *It was* [previously] *very much a done-to climate*, the ethos in the school, and staff thinking they knew best. (Headteacher, p 329, italics in original)[209]

> I think in terms of people coming onto the [action group] team, initially it was very positive and we had, in fact we had too many people probably. I got as diverse [a] range as possible, there were quite a few students who were keen. [It wasn't just] goody-goody high attainers. (Assistant headteacher, p 329)[209]

Students reported that they valued the opportunity action groups provided to express their views and highlight problems. Action groups provided a safe space to do this. As one student described:

> I was able to speak from my own point of view, not just like statistics and what was on a piece of paper. Because I was able to like … I started … talking about my own experiences. The teachers were acknowledging

it and ... It kind of felt good because it's like ... it's not me having to shout at a teacher or like I want to do this ... It's difficult for a teacher with a class of thirty or more students. (p 992)[208]

Students also said that teachers listened to their views even when they disagreed with them. For example, one student said: 'That was good because we didn't feel intimidated by the teachers. Not that you felt intimidated before, but you didn't feel like ... you could say something, all the teachers would listen ... everyone put across their own views with no arguments or anything' (p 992).[208]

Usefulness of needs assessment

The students and staff on action groups whom we interviewed attested to how the needs assessment report could inform change both by giving fresh impetus for and evidence about topics already known to be important and by identifying new priorities. As a headteacher explained:

Did we believe the results? Yes, probably. [The survey found that] they were feeling quite negative about the school and I think that's because they were getting lots of negative messages again, and it was because we were enforcing them: 'you are the worst year group in the school, your behaviour is terrible, stop behaving so badly', all from a negative perspective. We're hoping that the second round of the results comes back better and shows improvement, because what we've tried to do, alongside all of this work, is to keep re-emphasising the positive. (p 330)[209]

Staff who sat on action groups often reported that they used the reports as evidence when making a case to school leaders for change. For example, in one school, the report was used by staff to lobby leaders on behalf of students whose previously voiced concerns had not been acted on. As the assistant headteacher explained: 'It certainly gave me some ammunition that I can say, "Well this is ... this is proven because the kids have actually said this. So we need to move forward with it"' (p 989).[208]

Value of external facilitation

Staff across schools commented that the external facilitator was important for supporting decision-making, as illustrated by the following quote from a teacher:

So working with a facilitator from outside, that has been quite good at making it ... just more ... focused and more effective in that way. Because I think people in schools have really, really good ideas but again, because of the time, you tend to let things slip. Whereas this has kind of imposed a formality to it which means you have to keep to deadlines and move things forward. (p 991)[208]

Locally decided actions

Schools often made major changes as a result of the action group. For example, our lead facilitator described how some schools revised their behaviour policy:

> They changed their behaviour policy ... their rewards policy was completely overhauled ... and that was as a result of the fact that a lot of, well, most of the pupils in the action group felt unrewarded and didn't value the rewards that they were given, and they certainly didn't perceive them to be motivational. And also, [regarding] the staff, a real issue of inconsistency came up and a lot of staff felt that people were rewarded inappropriately, so that was why that part of the behaviour policy was altered. So that was the key thing, that was the key policy that was changed. (p 332)[209]

One staff member on a school action team explained that the time for tutor groups was extended as a result of the action group:

> Now tutor time is very short here. Now this is one of the things that's come out of the action group ... So it looks like we're going to have a much bigger tutor time where we're going to be able to implement a programme through the year, and I would definitely envisage that SEAL [social and emotional aspects of learning] would be a part of that ... If it's not SEAL itself it would be SEAL related, because we're looking at their emotional development within tutor time and checking in and checking out. (p 333)[209]

Other actions included: cascading training in restorative practice to other staff; holding assemblies on restorative practice; increasing or reorienting staff patrols of hallways between lessons to prevent or address problematic behaviours; instituting safe spaces within the school; offering more after-school clubs; providing drop-in services to improve engagement; funding new specialist staff to work with students to improve mental health and wellbeing; decorating the schools with informational or motivational posters; and displaying student work.[208]

Usefulness of restorative practice

The restorative practice also proved feasible and acceptable. It was widely regarded as extremely useful for dealing with behavioural problems and conflicts. The presence of a staff member who championed the use of restorative practice was critical to its broader use. It was used by most of those staff who had attended the in-depth training. However, some of these staff expressed frustration that not all of their colleagues were immediately adopting restorative practice. Where it was used, staff felt that it allowed them to resolve problems more easily because they would focus on restoring relationships rather than becoming bogged down in culpability. As a teacher in one school explained:

> And before I found we were spending a lot of time in 'Billy said (a), Johnny said (b)'. And we're arguing about (a) and (b) forever and ever and you probably never get to the end of it. And now Billy gets to give his view, Johnny gets to give his view, and then we move on to how we're going to move on and what this is going to look like in the future. (p 65)[207]

In other schools, restorative practice was used primarily as a strategy to manage classroom and learning behaviour. This often took the form of requiring a restorative conversation before readmitting to the classroom a student who had been removed because they breached expected norms of behaviour.

Students in general reported positive experiences of restorative practice. Several students told us in interviews that restorative practice could improve relationships where these had been subject to conflict. Students did not necessarily leave conferences as friends, but they were better able to manage their relationships. As one student described:

> I thought it [restorative conference] was useful because if we wouldn't have had it there would have been many, many, many more problems … It's not like it's completely gone. It's not, because there's still a bit of tension between all of us … It's not as big as it used to be. (p 65)[207]

Evaluation of impacts

The randomised controlled trial

The findings from the process evaluation help tell us whether Learning Together was feasible and acceptable. They give us some insights into how the intervention might work. But they don't tell us whether it actually did work in terms of preventing bullying and other risk behaviours or promoting students' health. Our study used other methods to assess this. The whole intervention was evaluated using a randomised controlled trial,[167] which is an experimental design aiming to assess the impacts of an intervention. This uses methods that aim to distinguish the 'signal' of intervention effects from the 'noise' of other, confounding effects.

To explain why randomised controlled trials are so useful, let's start by thinking through the different ways we might measure the effects of an intervention. We could have evaluated Learning Together by recruiting a group of schools to deliver the intervention and then assessing whether there were lower rates of bulling reported in student surveys done after the intervention compared to before the intervention. This is called a before-and-after study design. But if we found a reduction using this design, we would not know if this was due to the intervention or whether it was actually due to the students getting older, schools changing in ways that had nothing to do with our intervention or national trends that also had nothing to do with our intervention.

To take account of these other trends, we could compare our before-and-after results in the schools delivering Learning Together with before-and-after results in schools that chose not to deliver Learning Together. This is what is known as a quasi-experimental study design. Such schools would carry on with their normal practice rather than delivering Learning Together. We might find a trend towards lower bullying in our 'intervention' schools compared to our 'comparison' schools. However, this apparently positive result might have nothing to do with Learning Together. It might instead reflect the fact that the kinds of schools opting to deliver Learning Together happened to be more effective schools or have less troublesome students than the schools acting as comparisons. One way to address this problem would be to try to match schools in the intervention and comparison groups. We might have tried to match our intervention and comparison schools on their exam results or on the poverty of their students. This would have been possible and might have made for a fairer comparison. However, matching cannot address every factor that might affect our results. For example, the schools recruited into the study to deliver Learning Together might have been more determined to tackle bullying than schools recruited to be comparisons. It is impossible to know and measure all the potentially 'confounding' factors.

This seems like an intractable problem that means we can never know if school-based (or any other) interventions are effective. But the randomised controlled trial offers a simple and elegant solution to this problem. It is easiest to explain this design by describing our randomised controlled trial of Learning Together.

At the start, we recruited 40 schools to the study, using emails and phone calls to state secondary schools in southern England. We told schools that they had a fifty-fifty chance of receiving Learning Together or becoming a control school. We conducted baseline surveys of students at the end of their first year of secondary school. We then randomly allocated 20 of the schools to the intervention group and 20 to the control group. Those randomly allocated to the intervention group received the training, materials and facilitation and set about implementing the intervention. Those randomly allocated to the control group carried on with their normal activities. We carried out follow-up surveys of students in all 40 schools two and three years after the baseline survey. The three-year survey was to assess whether we had an impact on bullying and health outcomes. The two-year survey was to assess whether we had an impact on student engagement and belonging, which our theory suggested was the route to the impacts on bullying and health outcomes.

Our analyses compared trends in bullying and other outcomes between the intervention and control schools. Unlike matching, randomisation tends to generate intervention and control groups that resemble one another in terms of all the factors that might affect the rate of bullying and other outcomes at follow-up. This includes factors we know are important as well as unknown factors. So any differences in results between the intervention and control schools should represent what the intervention adds to all the other influences: its impact. Russell Viner and I led the evaluation of the effects of Learning Together on bullying, aggression, and substance use and all the other health outcomes described earlier. An independent team from the University of Manchester was funded by the Educational Endowment Foundation to examine the impact of Learning Together on academic attainment. This was done by obtaining government data on how well the cohort of students did in their final GCSE exams.

The main results

As evaluators, we are used to our studies finding that interventions have little or no impacts. In our experience, interventions rarely have the transformative effects that their developers hope for. We had previously been shocked at the finding from our evaluation of the Young People's Development Programme that this programme had actually been harmful (see Chapter 5). We were therefore a little pessimistic about the chances of Learning Together being effective. This pessimism was deepened because it had become clear during the trial that the social and emotional skills lessons had been poorly implemented. It was also clear that schools varied in their commitment to the programme, some schools really valuing our approach and delivering it thoroughly but other schools not delivering all components well.

Our statisticians, Liz Allen, Charles Opondo and Jo Sturgess, undertook their analyses during the summer of 2017. I remember returning from my family holiday with a feeling of trepidation that normally accompanies these analyses. As I emerged from my local tube station in London, I received a call from Liz with a slight sense of dread. The normally calm Professor Allen sounded somewhat excited. To my surprise and delight, the trial reported consistently positive findings. The intervention reduced bullying (but not aggression) as our primary outcome. In terms of our secondary outcomes, it reduced smoking tobacco, drinking alcohol, getting drunk, using drugs and experiencing psychological problems.[167] It increased mental wellbeing and health-related quality of life. These benefits were not apparent at the two-year follow-up but appeared, as we had hypothesised, only at the three-year follow-up. This made sense because the intervention needed time first to change the school as an organisation and then for these changes to benefit students. The evidence of effectiveness in promoting mental health was especially encouraging given the suggestion from observational studies that schools make only a small difference to students' mental health compared to larger differences for violence and substance use.[109] The trial found benefits in terms of both improved student mental wellbeing and reduced psychological difficulties.

Our economic analysis, led by Rosa Legood, found that the intervention was highly cost-effective and very cheap, in the lowest cost category for UK school interventions.[167] The results from the Manchester team, led by Michael Wigelsworth, came more slowly as they had to wait for the students to take their exams and for the government to share these data. But there was more good news: Learning Together improved attainment in GCSE academic exams.

Further analyses

We carried out further analyses to examine which schools and students benefited most.[167] Statistical analyses told us that the intervention was equally effective for disadvantaged and more advantaged students. They told us it was more effective for boys than girls in terms of its effects on quality of life, psychological problems, mental wellbeing, regular smoking, ever having drunk alcohol, bullying perpetration and contact with police (though not for the primary outcome of bullying victimisation). And they told us it was more effective for students who had been bullied at baseline in terms of there being even bigger positive effects for these students on bullying and psychological problems, quality of life and wellbeing. We were surprised and disappointed that the intervention was not *more* effective for disadvantaged than advantaged students, given the suggestion in the theory of human functioning and school organisation that actions to improve student engagement and belonging are more likely to benefit disadvantaged students. But at least the intervention had been *as* effective for these students as it was for more advantaged students (which is often not the case[210]). We interpreted the greater effectiveness for boys as reflecting the greater visibility to schools of trouble involving boys so that this was prioritised in their responses. We were delighted to see a greater benefit for students who had experienced bullying at baseline.

We also carried out exploratory analyses of the effects of Learning Together on other outcomes, finding evidence for the intervention also achieving reductions over three years in students' cyberbullying perpetration, observation of aggression by other students, truancy, participation in school disciplinary procedures and e-cigarette use.[211]

Finally, G.J. Melendez-Torres led further statistical analyses to understand how Learning Together achieved its impacts on bullying. We found that at baseline, students tended to belong to one of the following categories: bullying victims; aggression perpetrators; extreme perpetrators; and neither victims nor perpetrators. In intervention schools compared to control schools, fewer of the extreme perpetrators stayed in that category, more of the extreme perpetrators moved down to the category of aggression perpetrators, and more of the aggression perpetrators moved to become neither victims nor perpetrators.[212]

These results were more encouraging than we could ever have hoped at the start of the study. Learning Together helped all of the schools achieve significant benefits for their students. This occurred without any changes in national educational policy. Schools remained highly focused on attainment, and many staff shared with us their hope that Learning Together could help them achieve improvements in this, which was confirmed by Michael Wigelsworth's analysis of GCSE results.

What happened next

Our findings suggested the value of scaling up Learning Together for all schools in England. Despite our best efforts to disseminate our findings and influence policy, and despite the results being so unusually positive, Learning Together was not scaled up in England. The results did inform policy in Scotland and Wales, and the intervention was taken up by some schools and some local authorities in England.

We were of course disappointed by the lack of scale-up in England. But I believe that the most important finding of our study is not about the benefits of Learning Together as a single, specific programme. Instead, our results are most important in terms of what they say about the general ways in which schools can benefit their students by disrupting the three toxic mechanisms of educational disengagement, lack of belonging, and fear and anxiety. Learning Together is being further developed within some new research studies. In one study, Learning Together has been adapted to amplify its already significant impacts on mental health; the new intervention is called Learning Together for Mental Health. The needs assessment survey and the needs report for schools have been refined so that these assess various areas of mental health, such as anxiety, depression, eating disorders and self-harm. Additionally, schools receive a menu of evidence-based actions that they can take to promote mental health in the specific areas of need identified for their school. Learning Together is also being adapted for piloting in English primary schools; this intervention is called Learning Together Primary Schools and is led by Neisha Sundaram. The adapted intervention uses a simplified action group process suitable for younger children.

Conclusion

This chapter has described how schools, in theory and in practice, can be transformed to disrupt the toxic mechanisms of educational disengagement, lack of school belonging, and fear and anxiety in order to promote young people's health. It described the theory of human functioning and school organisation as the most detailed and comprehensive theory of how schools can promote student health. It went on to describe the Learning Together intervention, which was informed by this theory and was feasible and acceptable to deliver and which benefited students in terms of reduced bulling, reduced substance use, improved mental health and improved educational attainment. The results were particularly encouraging for mental health given the suggestion from observational studies that school effects on this might be quite small. Learning Together is, in fact, not an isolated success, as we see in the next chapter. The remainder of the book looks at other similar interventions, explores in more detail how and for whom such interventions work and draws out the implications of this for educational policy.

7

International examples of effective school detox

Introduction

Just because an intervention is effective in one place or time or with one population does not mean it will be effective elsewhere. There has recently been something of a crisis of replication in the fields of social science, medicine, psychology and economics, where the results of one study are not always confirmed by replications of the study in similar or different settings.[213] [214] However, in the case of school interventions, the evidence seems to suggest that interventions similar to Learning Together, which modify school organisation to promote engagement, belonging and support to benefit student health, have been effective in a very broad range of places, times and populations.[215] Similar interventions have had broadly similar effects in a diverse range of countries, including Australia, India, Uganda and the US.

Interventions that informed Learning Together

Learning Together was strongly informed by the US Aban Aya and the Australian Gatehouse interventions and by the scientists who led the development and testing of these interventions, Brian Flay in the US and George Patton in Australia, both of whom sadly died in recent years.

The **Aban Aya** youth project, led by Brian Flay, involved changes to the school environment coupled with social skills lessons. It was evaluated in Chicago middle schools serving largely Black, highly disadvantaged students.[216] The intervention aimed to reduce risk behaviours by 'rebuilding the village' to enhance students' sense of belonging and community and increase social support. It was strongly informed by theories suggesting that enhancing relationships and cultural pride could reduce aggression, substance use and other risk behaviours.[217] Aban Aya involved a standardised process of institutional change. Schools set up a local task force comprising staff, students, parents and local residents. These bodies reviewed and revised school policies relating to young people's health, behaviour and school ethos. Schools aimed to build bridges with local community organisations and businesses. Teachers reoriented teaching so that this was more interactive and culturally appropriate. A trial found that Aban Aya reduced violence, bullying, truancy and school suspension among boys but not girls.[216]

The **Gatehouse Project**, led by George Patton and Lyndal Bond, was developed and trialled in Victoria state, Australia.[218,219] It aimed to promote students' mental and physical health by changing high school cultures to promote students' security, self-regard and positive communication with staff and other students. The intervention lasted for two academic years. Schools used surveys to assess students' needs and views on priorities. Schools instituted action teams comprising staff and students, and these were facilitated by an external 'critical friend' – a professional with experience in schools or other children's services. These action groups reviewed the survey data to determine priorities. They also reviewed and revised existing policies to promote a more positive school environment. Teachers were trained in, and students were taught, social and emotional skills. The Gatehouse Project was evaluated using a randomised controlled trial and was found to reduce a range of health risk behaviours, including early sexual initiation and substance use.[218,219] Like Learning Together, effects grew over time as the intervention transformed schools as institutions.[219]

These interventions both used groups involving staff and students to drive change in school environments. The interventions had impacts on outcomes such as violence and substance use. Like Learning Together, the Gatehouse intervention brought benefits that built up over time.

My colleagues and I read about Aban Aya and the Gatehouse Project as we took our first steps in developing the intervention that would eventually become Learning Together. We emailed Brian Flay and George Patton for advice and both engaged with us with great generosity. They advised in detail how to develop and evaluate these sorts of whole-school change interventions. Lyndal Bond moved to the UK to work at the University of Glasgow and joined our team to develop, pilot and then trial Learning Together. The intervention and its evaluation were much improved as a result of all this advice.

The **Seattle Social Development Project** was a study in US elementary schools that preceded and informed both Aban Aya and Gatehouse. The intervention aimed to reduce student risk behaviours by increasing student bonding to school; this was via teacher training, parent education and student education in social skills. Teachers received training to change their instructional methods in three ways: by taking proactive steps to deliver more engaging classroom lessons; by using more interactive teaching methods; and by organising students into cooperative learning groups. Parents received advice and support about parenting to enable them to better support their students' engagement in learning. Students were taught a curriculum focused on developing their cognitive and social skills. A quasi-experimental study compared long-term outcomes among students in schools allocated to receive different levels of the intervention. This reported benefits for students receiving the full intervention in terms of reduced violence, heavy drinking, early sexual initiation, multiple sexual partners, pregnancy and sexually transmitted infections as well as higher academic commitment, school attachment and educational attainment.[220,221]

Other interventions transforming schools to promote health

As we proceeded with the randomised controlled trial of Learning Together, we became aware of other interventions taking a broadly similar approach and addressing a range of health outcomes that had been or were being evaluated across diverse sites and populations.

The **Cooperative Learning** programme was delivered in US middle schools. It aimed to introduce progressive group-based learning to schools. This approach included reciprocal teaching among students, peer tutoring and collaborative reading groups. These aimed to enable students to help each other learn in small groups. The activities were developed based on principles of positive interdependence so that individuals could achieve their own goals only if their group achieved its goals. This might involve a single goal for a group (goal interdependence), students being rewarded only if everyone reached a certain level or goal (reward interdependence), each member having different materials that they must share to achieve their goal (resource interdependence), each member having a specific role to play (role interdependence) or each member having a specific task to complete (task interdependence) as part of the team. These processes aimed to promote mutual support among students, instead of competition and isolation. The approach also involved coaching for students in using collaborative social skills. A trial found that the intervention reduced rates of bullying, stress, alcohol use and emotional problems.[222–224] There was evidence that the effects on some of these outcomes was mediated by improved peer relatedness.[225]

The **Good School Toolkit** includes changes to discipline systems, improvements to the physical environment, student involvement in decisions and communal celebrations in primary schools serving adolescents in Uganda.[226] Use of the toolkit involves six steps, completed in sequence, with over 60 different activities for teachers, students and school administrators. These activities focus on topics such as improving the school environment, improving teaching and learning, building mutual respect, creating accountability and staff learning non-violent methods of discipline. The intervention works with teachers, administrators, students and parents to change ideas and attitudes. Staff, students and administrators set school-wide goals, formulate action plans, develop empathy by facilitating reflection on experiences of violence and provide opportunities to practise new skills. Staff and student 'protagonists' lead activities with other staff and students in their school, encouraging them to form, lead and join groups for various intervention activities. Students participate actively and form committees and groups related to different activities. Schools are encouraged to celebrate successful implementation. Student and staff improve the school site by painting murals on school walls and posting codes of conduct in visible areas. A randomised controlled trial led by Karen Devries found that the intervention reduced staff and peer violence against students.

The **Healthy Youth Places** intervention involved students and staff in US middle schools developing local plans for increasing opportunities for physical activity and healthy eating at school.[227] This aimed to develop the capacity of school staff and students to ensure school environments featured opportunities for healthy eating and physical activity. This occurred via school coordinators facilitating youth-led school advocacy groups, known as 'change teams', also involving school staff, which were the hub of intervention activities at the school. Local capacity to participate in intervention activities was enabled through training for staff and students on leadership skills. The facilitation of the youth-led school advocacy groups by the site coordinators was supported by a training programme for young people in school change. A randomised controlled trial reported that the intervention generated increases in vigorous physical activity and moderate to vigorous physical activity. The intervention did not have effects on any outcomes relating to healthy eating other than students' self-efficacy to eat five to seven portions of fruit and vegetables per day and group norms that were supportive of fruit and vegetable consumption.

The **SEHER** (Strengthening evidence base on school-based interventions for promoting adolescent health) programme was implemented in secondary schools in Bihar, a very poor state in India. The overall approach used a coordinating group involving staff and students, changes to discipline and other policies, improved teaching and various communal activities.[228] Whole-school activities aimed to address hygiene, bullying, mental health, substance use, reproductive and sexual health, gender and violence, rights and responsibilities, and study skills. Each school formed a School Health Promotion Committee involving administrators, parents, teachers and students. The committee managed and monitored the programme. The committee also considered priorities identified by students via a speak-out letterbox. The committee was supported by an intervention lead, who facilitated assemblies and other activities, a magazine, competitions for students and policies on zero tolerance to bullying and substance use. These policies were developed with staff and students in the School Health Promotion Committee meetings. Students from each class elected a representative for a peer group meeting, which met monthly to discuss the topic of the month and student concerns, develop a plan of action and assist in organising the whole-school activities. The intervention lead ran a workshop on effective study skills for students and supportive and non-exclusionary disciplinary practices for teachers. The intervention lead also provided counselling or referrals for students in need. The study involved a three-arm randomised controlled trial, led by Vikram Patel, Sachin Shinde and Helen Weiss. In one arm of the trial, the intervention was led by a teacher and in another, by a lay counsellor. The third arm was the control group. This trial found that the lay counsellor version of SEHER was associated with reductions in depression as well as violence victimisation and perpetration. There were also improvements in school climate, attitude towards gender equity and knowledge of reproductive and sexual health.[228] There was some evidence that the effects of SEHER on depression were mediated by an impact on school climate.[229] No such benefits were detected for the teacher-led arm.

These interventions all addressed student engagement in learning, sense of belonging in a school community and/or sense of support and safety. Common components included using needs assessment to determine local priorities, involving students and staff in collaborative decision-making, revising school policies to better support students, reorienting school discipline systems and promoting communal experiences to build a sense of collective identity and belonging. These helped the intervention address local needs, ensure student voices were heard, ensure talk translated into actions and improve relationships between staff and students.

Simpler interventions to promote student belonging

Two other types of intervention from the US aim to address student sense of school belonging, engagement in learning and anxiety, not via the sorts of elaborate processes of school environment change used in the interventions mentioned earlier but by brief interventions for students and staff. The Student Belonging intervention was led by Greg Walton, and the Teacher Empathetic Discipline intervention was led by Jason Okonofua.

The **Student Belonging** intervention aims to increase sense of school belonging and school engagement among high school students via two brief classroom sessions[230] to reduce anxiety about school belonging.[231] The intervention presents students with a booklet providing survey results and stories from older students conveying that challenges and worries about school are normal and improve with time. The theory of change is that students are helped to think about their experiences and how these reflect processes of change rather than indicating fixed personal limitations. This gives students a more adaptive narrative to interpret adversities, helping them sustain a sense of belonging, stay academically engaged and build more trusting relationships and interactions with teachers. In a randomised trial, the intervention reduced disciplinary incidents and academic test anxiety, and it improved sense of school belonging and improved educational attainment, with the greatest benefits for male, Black students. The intervention cost was $1.35 per student per year.

The **Teacher Empathetic Discipline** intervention focuses on high school teachers, helping them take a more empathic approach to misbehaving students via two sessions of teacher-directed online reading with students and a reflection exercise. The theory of change involves teachers reflecting on the opportunities they have to help students grow and learn, even when students misbehave, and listening to students and taking an empathetic approach to understanding and responding to them, thereby sustaining positive relationships and building student trust in school staff as well as a sense of school belonging. The intervention uses narratives and written reflection exercises to represent this approach, informed by research, as normative, optimal and intuitive. Teachers are asked to reflect on what they have reviewed and their own experiences and to use that to write advice to an imagined new teacher to help them navigate relationships with students. This task helps participants articulate a psychological message for themselves, connect it to their own experience and use it in the future. An initial randomised controlled trial reported fewer suspensions for violence and other antisocial behaviour among students aged 11–13, with no differences by ethnicity or gender.[232] Intervention costs were very low, involving only teacher time for training.

The Student Belonging intervention and the Empathetic Discipline intervention have been subject to replication studies in the US, and these have shown sustained effectiveness in addressing school belonging, disciplinary incidents, suspensions, attendance, social support and educational attainment.[230,233–235] For example, a large replication trial for the Empathetic Discipline initiative yielded a similar reduction in suspensions for violence and other antisocial behaviour as found in the initial trial, with effects greatest for ethnic minority and educationally disabled students and reductions persisting through the next school year.[233] While studies with high school students have not examined impacts on general health, studies of very similar interventions with university students report significant impacts on general health, mental wellbeing and medical attendances.[236,237] The consistent impact of these interventions is particularly notable given their simplicity and brevity. This has been attributed to the 'psychologically precise' way in which they target student and teacher determinants of student sense of school belonging and risk behaviours.[231,238] At the time of writing, I am planning a replication study to assess whether these interventions might work in England and whether they might be effective in preventing bullying and promoting mental health.

The evaluations of the initiatives described in this chapter together suggest that interventions aiming to modify schools in ways that address engagement in learning, sense of belonging in a school community and student support can bring about various benefits across a range of places, times and populations. These include reductions in risk behaviours, such as violence, bullying, alcohol use and lack of physical activity. They include mental health benefits, such as reduced stress, emotional problems and depression. They also include improvements in sexual health outcomes, such as attitude towards gender equity and knowledge of reproductive and sexual health. And they include better educational outcomes related to, for example, school climate, truancy and school suspension. The interventions worked across a variety of places, spanning Africa, Asia, Europe, North America and Oceania. They spanned populations ranging from children attending primary schools providing basic learning through to middle and high schools with populations and settings varying hugely in terms of population needs, school infrastructures, teacher expertise and education policy.

A systematic review of the evidence

Our awareness of these interventions encouraged us in the belief that this sort of intervention had enormous potential to improve young people's health, and it also shone a light on the general mechanisms by which schools could be modified to do this by disrupting the three toxic mechanisms of educational disengagement, lack of belonging, and fear and anxiety. Nonetheless, as public health scientists, we are aware of the risk that our belief in this type of intervention can potentially bias us in terms of which studies we read and what conclusions we draw from them. There is an ignominious history of researchers drawing incorrect conclusions about the effectiveness of interventions by allowing such bias to affect how they review the literature.[239] The systematic review was developed as the solution to this. We decided that the next step was to conduct a systematic review in this area.

Systematic reviews to minimise bias

Systematic reviews aim to bring a scientific, comprehensive and impartial approach to bear on the reviewing of scientific literature. Systematic reviewers start by defining a precise, answerable question and setting out inclusion criteria that indicate what sorts of evidence are pertinent to rigorously answering the question. They then mount a comprehensive search to find as much of the relevant evidence as possible. The reviewers define in advance how they will grade the quality of the evidence and how they will weight this in their analysis. The reviewers then analyse the evidence found. Some of this analysis is statistical. The statistical results of multiple studies can be pooled to, in effect, construct a larger virtual study, known as a statistical meta-analysis. This can be useful, but there is also a risk that the meta-analysis will inappropriately combine studies of very different interventions done in different places with different populations and/or using different methods. So systematic reviews also involve what are called narrative analyses. These describe the different results of studies in words, being attentive to such differences.

Systematic review of interventions aiming to build student commitment to school to promote health

My team and I carried out a systematic review focused on interventions aiming to prevent substance use and violence in schools, which are important public health outcomes we know to be associated with lack of school engagement or belonging at the level of the individual student and at the level of the school. Our review sought to examine the effects on substance use and violence of interventions that promote student commitment to school (in terms of educational engagement or school belonging).

We defined our inclusion criteria so that eligible studies were evaluations of whole-school interventions aiming to reduce violence or substance (tobacco, alcohol, other drugs) use among students aged 5–18 years in schools by modifying teaching to increase engagement in learning, enhancing student–staff relationships, revising school policies, encouraging student volunteering or involving parents in school. We searched for such studies using a very comprehensive strategy involving electronic databases, reading reference lists and consulting experts in the field. This identified 62,742 studies. We carefully screened all of these to determine if we should include them in the review or not. We identified 48 studies that reported on the effectiveness of pertinent interventions in preventing substance use or violence, and 16 studies that conducted process evaluations to explore what factors helped or hindered delivery. We then assessed the quality of the included studies using existing checklists. Finally, we analysed the findings both by pooling the results of studies, looking at similar outcomes, and by narratively synthesising studies.

Review findings

The statistical meta-analyses were led by my colleague G.J. Melendez-Torres.[240] These found that interventions of this sort brought about significant reductions in violence perpetration and victimisation up to one year later and also more than one year later. The meta-analyses also found that these interventions led to significant reductions in overall measures of substance use up to one year later and more than one year later. Our narrative synthesis compared and contrasted the results of particular studies.[240] We found some evidence that improvements in student commitment to school mediated the effects of the interventions on health outcomes.

The synthesis of process evaluations was led by Ruth Ponsford.[241] This found that a number of factors affected implementation. School staff were more likely to understand what they needed to do to implement an intervention when they were provided with good materials and support. Whether these staff then committed to delivery was affected by whether they thought the interventions could be integrated with existing school practices and locally tailored or able to build on existing work. Interventions that provided data on local students' needs achieved good staff buy-in. Staff were also more likely to commit when they perceived the external providers involved as credible and experienced. Students were more likely to see interventions as acceptable if the these offered them opportunities for active roles or ways to express their views. School leaders were more likely to commit to deliver an intervention when it addressed an issue they were already interested in tackling and when there was already a recognition of the need for change within a school.

School staff and students worked together to deliver interventions better when the intervention was seen as locally workable, fitting with timetables and providing clear guidance. Interventions that included 'action groups' helped solidify collective action. Interventions that had obviously synergistic components (such as changes in practices supported by changes in policy) were implemented more successfully. Whether or not staff came together to deliver interventions also depended on their having the time, budgets, authority and connections to support this. Action groups enabled members to keep implementation under review and determine what further work was needed. Such reviews could give participants the permission and resources to try different things and persist with those that worked.

This systematic review did not examine all the various health outcomes that interventions of this type might address. It also struggled to analyse studies of often quite different interventions in different places and with different populations. Nonetheless, the positive findings do suggest that interventions of this sort are likely to have wide applicability and value.

Conclusion

Learning Together is not an isolated example of an intervention that improves young people's health by transforming school environments. It was strongly informed by the Aban Aya and Gatehouse initiatives in the US and Australia, respectively. These in turn were influenced by the Seattle Social Development Project. An array of school transformation interventions have been evaluated across settings spanning Africa, Asia, Europe, North America and Oceania. These have achieved student benefits in the domains of violence, substance use, mental health, physical activity, sexual health and various educational outcomes. They support the finding from Learning Together that changes to the school environment can improve mental health as well as reduce violence and substance use. They extend the findings from Learning Together in that they suggest school environment change can benefit students in terms of physical activity and sexual health. A systematic review of the effects of school-based interventions that promote student commitment to school (in terms of educational engagement or school belonging) found that these tended to reduce both violence and substance use in the short and the long term. The next chapter explores the question of what works, for whom and where. It examines how interventions might be adapted to best meet the needs of different populations.

8

What works, for whom and where

Introduction

In Chapters 6 and 7, we saw how interventions aiming to increase engagement, belonging, and safety and support in schools can benefit students across a range of health and educational outcomes. This chapter explores how school context, country context and the specific health outcomes being addressed affect what schools need to do.

School context

Different schools have different cultures, different capacities for action, different pressures and different priorities. So when embarking on change, they are likely to need to start from different places and do different things.

Factors affecting delivery

Schools will vary in how hard they find it to deliver health interventions. With Lauren Herlitz, Laurence Blanchard and other colleagues, I have undertaken a couple of systematic reviews looking at what factors affect this.[196,242] We know from these that implementation is much easier if school staff have the confidence to feel that they are able to deliver the intervention and if they believe in its value. Implementation is also more likely when an intervention has the support of committed colleagues and senior leaders and when it aligns with national policy. Implementation is likely to be sustained if staff can see a rapid positive impact on students' engagement and wellbeing. Sustained delivery is also more likely if interventions can be adapted to existing school systems and routines.

Implementation is harder when there is a norm within a school of prioritising educational outcomes over student health and wellbeing. It is also harder where there are time and resource constraints, a lack of staff training and a high staff turnover.

Different approaches for different schools: evidence from Learning Together

Because schools differ in how able they are to implement interventions, the level of ambition a school aims for in delivering an intervention needs to align with its capacity. Learning Together was designed to allow local tailoring by enabling the action group in each school to choose actions they would take based on evidence from reports on student needs. However, our evaluation led us to conclude that there should be even more fundamental tailoring than this, with schools also factoring in their capacity when deciding what to deliver. Our evaluation found that different schools focused on different aspects of the intervention depending on their capacity. As a result, different mechanisms of action were triggered in different schools.[243]

Qualitative evidence

The first mechanism of action triggered by the intervention involved improving relationships between staff and students, with this resulting in improved student engagement and belonging (as set out in our theory of change). Emily Warren and I first explored this in interviews and focus groups with staff and students. These suggest that action groups provided a space for students and staff to share views and listen to others. As one staff member described:

> I think that the students … enjoy the fact that we're doing something like this so they can be involved in it and that they can actually have their voice heard, that they can feel safe at school, that they can feel engaged with the teachers, that they can feel they're listened to.[243]

Through exposure, in a nonconfrontational setting, to teachers describing how student misbehaviour affected them, students learnt to view teachers as people with feelings. One teacher commented: 'I suppose in some respects the students need to know that, ultimately, you're a human being. Because I think they forget that we're a human being and we have feelings.'[243]

Collaborating with teachers in the action group could help students build relationships with staff. This was especially important for those students who had been selected because of their disengagement with school. Students in a focus group described how relationships improved through the action group because they felt more respected: 'Much more respectful … yeah, they treat you with the same amount of respect as they would do their colleagues.'[243] Better relationships could motivate students to work harder, as described by one student: 'If you have a bond with your teacher … you want to do well for the teacher because you feel like she's paid attention to you and gave her respect. And the way you can respect her back is by working hard.'[243]

The action group could also enable students to take on new roles contributing to the school community. For example, students on the action group at the St Anselm school were asked to interpret the findings from the needs report. In doing so, they were accorded an expert role in contrast to their usual role of passive learner. One teacher commented:

> [Analysing the needs report] has then really highlighted to us as staff in school where we need to be focusing some particular work with the students …. And then we've obviously taken a lot of advice and input from the students as to how they would like things to change in the school. So … students [are] feeling like they're actually having an input.[243]

These mechanisms would have only limited impacts if they were restricted to students in the action group, but at least in some schools this was not the case. Many students were recruited to action groups because of their lack of prior engagement and their involvement in antisocial behaviour. When these students had positive experiences in the group, this could catalyse a broader change across the school, as described by one teacher:

> We have a boy … [a] proper naughty boy. But he has shown such maturity in the final part of his year-11 and he's been, I think, an outstanding student in year-12. But all the kids know who he is or they know of the local family. And so, if he's on board [with the action group], that sends a really important message. And I think that is critical.[243]

But such mechanisms were contingent on action groups being run well, and this depended on the school having the necessary organisational capacity and, ideally, at least the beginnings of a culture of inclusivity even before the intervention began. It was noticeable that in poorly managed schools or schools with more authoritarian cultures, the action groups were less successful.

The second mechanism of action triggered by the intervention involved curtailing conflict, with this having a direct effect by reducing bullying and violence (which was not explicitly set out in our initial theory of change, though it was implicitly assumed).[243] Restorative practice could work via increasing the sense of responsibility and empathy among perpetrators, leading to curtailment of bullying. Restorative practice could enable perpetrators to develop empathy for victims. In Harper's school, a student had persuaded a friend to use his mobile phone to take a photo of another boy on the toilet, which was then shared on social media. Initially, the student was unrepentant: '[During the meeting,] I was like, "I didn't really do anything" … Then they start staring at me. I'm like, "Don't look at me, I didn't do anything."'[243] But seeing how upset the victim was in the meeting encouraged the perpetrator to feel empathy and take responsibility:

And when we came in, it's just, like … at first I was laughing, because I just felt it was hilarious for him … someone to be taking the pictures of him in the toilet. But then when I just saw him there sitting down at this table and his eyes were all red from the tears … I just don't … it just came to me and just shocked me. That that could have happened to me really, it wouldn't be nice … I normally would have been moaning [about being punished], saying 'No' … But this time I actually felt what I had done was really wrong. It just makes me realise … I mean it's … just when I saw him sitting there in that state.[243]

Our interviews with staff suggest that for these mechanisms to be triggered, schools had to recognise that there was a need to address problem behaviour and there had to be widespread support for the use of restorative practice to do so.

Quantitative evidence

These insights into the mechanisms of action came from our qualitative research. As discussed in earlier chapters, qualitative research is strong on understanding experiences in depth, but it does not provide strong evidence of breadth of experience or causality.

So we conducted further statistical analyses, led by G.J. Melendez-Torres, to explore whether these potential mechanisms of action were occurring more generally and with what impacts.[244] These analyses suggest that in schools with certain advantages (strong management capacity, positive school climate and low rates of bullying at baseline), intervention effects on bullying, psychological problems and mental wellbeing were brought about via an intermediate effect on increased student belonging.

However, in schools lacking these initial advantages, the intervention still reduced bullying and improved mental health, but not via a pathway involving increased student belonging. We interpreted this as meaning that the former group of schools had the management capacity, supportive culture and bandwidth to deliver action groups really well. This could then trigger a mechanism whereby bullying was reduced and mental health improved via building student belonging. The latter group of schools lacked these advantages and had less bandwidth as a result of needing to deal with a high level of bullying. In these schools, restorative practice was the main focus for delivery, and this reduced bullying and improved mental health not via an improvement in student belonging, but more directly via curtailing conflict. We didn't have a direct measure of conflict curtailment in this latter group of schools, but it seems a safe bet that it occurred given that bullying and mental health were both successfully addressed and this was not via a mechanism involving improved student belonging.

Implications

We concluded that schools with strong management capacity, an already inclusive school culture and less need for firefighting high levels of bullying have the bandwidth to think big with work focused on building student participation and belonging. Struggling schools that have less management capacity and a less inclusive culture and which are facing more firefighting can start off smaller with work focused on curtailing conflict and improving relationships via restorative practice. As we take Learning Together forwards, we intend to build this into the guidance for schools on how to assess their capacity for change and, informed by this, what activities to concentrate on first. It might be that schools start off by focusing on restorative practice to get rates of bullying down and then start to implement action groups as their capacity for delivery improves. The previous chapter described the Student Belonging and Empathetic Discipline interventions, which aim to promote student engagement and belonging and reduce anxiety not by complex processes of school transformation but via brief interventions for, respectively, students and staff. Some schools lacking the time even to implement restorative practice may opt to start by delivering brief interventions such as these.

Country context

Interventions to modify school environments to benefit student health will also need to be tailored for different countries. Different countries (or in some cases, different regions of countries) will have different resources, cultures, and professional and institutional capacities and priorities, which means they will need to do different things. Schools in resource-poor settings might need to start off with simpler first steps. They might require more outside support or need to involve new personnel. For example, the previous chapter described the SEHER (Strengthening evidence base on school-based interventions for promoting adolescent health) programme, which was delivered in Bihar, a poor state in India. The intervention involved a coordinating group comprising staff and students, which led on changes to discipline and other policies and improved teaching and communal activities.[228] The evaluation found that this intervention was only effective in the arm of the trial where schools were provided with new practitioners to lead the work, as opposed to leaving this to school staff.

Evidence on preventing dating violence in different countries

Together with G.J Melendez-Torres and other colleagues, I conducted a systematic review examining the evidence on what school-based interventions are effective for preventing dating and relationship violence and gender-based violence.[245] Dating and relationship violence refers to abuse within relationships while gender-based violence also encompasses violence outside relationships. Our synthesis of studies examining the effects of interventions on gender-based violence found that to reduce this form of violence required the delivery of interventions that aimed to transform the school environment – for example, to improve engagement and belonging. However, we found that such interventions were only delivered effectively in high-income countries.

It is likely that in the studies in low- and middle-income countries, interventions to transform the school environment so as to prevent gender-based violence were simply too challenging to deliver given the lower capacity in schools. In contrast, the review found that dating and relationship violence could be prevented using simpler interventions that did not require transformation of school environment and hence were feasible across low-, middle- and high-income countries.[245] Synthesis of the evidence on mediation suggests that such interventions appeared to prevent victimisation and perpetration simply by encouraging students to regard such violence as unacceptable. Multiple studies indicated that effects on perpetration by boys were greater than on perpetration by girls. Some studies found that effects were greater among those who had previously been perpetrators of dating and relationship violence.

Our interpretation of this was that these interventions worked by emphasising the unacceptability of male perpetration of gender-based violence. This points to an important, more general lesson: while interventions that aim to transform schools to build student engagement, belonging, and safety and support are generally a feasible and effective approach to promoting young people's health, they will not always be feasible and may not always be necessary. Sometimes, simpler interventions may be just as effective. This point also comes up in the next section when considering school actions to address different health outcomes.

Specific outcomes

What schools need to do will also of course vary with the area of health to be addressed.

We have found that schools are more prepared to invest the time and other resources required when the intervention is focused on a problem that schools already recognise is common, serious and their responsibility, such as bullying. Schools seem to struggle to commit the necessary resources when interventions address topics that, though common and serious, they might not regard as a priority for them to address. This was the case, for example, when Rebecca Meiksin and I piloted a whole-school intervention called

Project Respect, addressing dating and relationship violence. This was a topic that schools did not see as a key priority at the time.[194] As a result, the intervention was delivered with low fidelity.

Subsequently, the issue of dating and relationship violence and other forms of sexual abuse rose up the list of schools' priorities. This occurred as a result of the Everyone's Invited initiative, which collected thousands of online testimonies about sexual abuse (see www.everyonesinvited.uk/). It suggested there were high rates of sexual abuse, including dating and relationship violence, in UK schools. This prompted Ofsted, the national school inspectorate for England, to undertake a review of sexual abuse in schools and colleges, which recommended that schools take whole-school actions to prevent abuse and harassment.[246] We are, at the time of writing, piloting a new intervention to address dating and relationship violence and other gender-based violence in schools. We hope that schools are now more likely to prioritise this sort of intervention.

We have also found that for some areas of health, schools recognise the importance of the topic and their role in addressing it but may not accept that this will require changes to the overall school environment. For example, Ruth Ponsford, Rebecca Meiksin and I, together with other colleagues, are evaluating the Positive Choices intervention to promote sexual health in English secondary schools.[247] This intervention involves some similar components to Learning Together – a needs assessment report informed by student surveys and a group comprising staff and students to coordinate the intervention. It also involves a relationships and sex education classroom curriculum, student-led campaigns on topics related to sexual health and a review of sexual health services in and around the school. The trial began in 2021, shortly after the teaching of relationships and sex education became a statutory requirement for all English schools.[176]

It has become clear in the course of the trial that schools in the intervention group are delivering the relationships and sex education lesson component much more consistently than the other components that focus on modifying the school environment. Interviews with staff suggest that many schools opted to participate in the trial because they were seeking a set of lesson materials to fulfil their obligation to teach relationships and sex education. The other elements were often not regarded as so important. The staff we spoke to often seemed to regard sexual health as a curriculum and not a school environment issue. This is despite there being evidence that sexual risk behaviour and teenage pregnancy are influenced by school experiences and school characteristics[23,104] and that interventions involving non-curriculum elements are an effective means to promote young people's sexual health.[248] This situation is almost exactly the reverse of the situation we found in some schools in the Learning Together trial, in which bullying was regarded as an issue requiring a school environment rather than a curriculum response.[167]

Our own and others' evaluations of interventions that have transformed school environments in order to address different health outcomes demonstrate that this is feasible and acceptable. Nonetheless, it is in some ways an odd thing to do to focus on specific health outcomes in order to motivate schools to undertaken major transformations of how they conduct their core business of engaging students in learning, involving them in a school community and protecting them from violence and anxiety. A great insight from public health research in general is that often the most effective way to promote health is to address the broader social determinants of health.[249] Effecting transformations in schools' core business is one example of this. But it can be challenging to persuade school staff, whose main focus is, quite rightly, student learning, to change how they do things in order to address health when this is not their main focus. I have certainly witnessed school staff being puzzled as to why we were encouraging them to change their approach to learning in order to, for example, promote sexual health or reduce bullying. I saw a similar look of puzzlement on the face of the minister of health in Barbados many years ago. I had been invited to advise Barbados' government on reducing coronary heart disease. Informed by the work of people such as Michael Marmot on economic inequality as a social determinant of health, I urged the health minister to lobby his colleagues in the finance ministry to work to reduce income inequality. The minister looked at me as though I were quite mad. He pivoted away from me to instead engage in discussion with another scientist present, who was instead advocating an increase in prescribing statins as an effective way to reduce coronary heart disease mortality.

Reflecting on these experiences suggests to me that it is implausible to use specific health outcomes as the main way to motivate schools to scale up interventions to promote student engagement in learning, belonging in a school community and protection in a safe and supportive environment. It is likely to be far more feasible to motivate schools to achieve such changes by orientating them towards goals that all schools would wish to sign up to.

First, rather than focusing on a different intervention for each specific health outcome, it would be better if such interventions helped schools to improve their students' health and wellbeing in a holistic way. Interventions might do so by taking a step-by-step and tailored approach. Schools might identify certain areas of health and wellbeing as initial priorities before going on to address other health outcomes. Interventions would phase in different intervention activities as schools go through a structured process of addressing different outcomes. We have seen that schools will have different starting points in terms of different capacities and different cultures, and a phased approach should also take this into account.

Second, and more fundamentally, it seems to me much more plausible to motivate schools to transform how they engage, involve and support students by focusing on achieving improvements in educational outcomes. It is highly likely that interventions of the sort described earlier will achieve educational benefits as well as health benefits. For some interventions, such as Learning Together, SEHER and the Seattle Social Development Programme, evaluations, discussed in the previous chapter, have provided evidence of benefits in terms of educational attendance,[167,216] engagement[167,220,228] and attainment.[167,220] Other interventions, such as cooperative group learning, have also demonstrated impacts on academic attainment.[250] There is similarly evidence from the US that coordinated school health programmes that feature multiple school-wide components are effective in improving educational attainment.[251] It is important that all future evaluations of interventions to modify the school environment to improve health also assess impacts on educational attainment, because this is likely to be such an important motivator for schools deciding whether to deliver such interventions.

Conclusion

Whole-school interventions offer a flexible and sustainable way for schools to promote health without needing lots of lesson time and new forms of expertise. Such interventions aim to transform how schools conduct their core business to disrupt the toxic mechanisms described in this book rather than merely attempting to compensate for these toxic mechanisms. School leaders will likely need to take different approaches, depending on the capacity within their school and the wider country as well as the specific outcomes to be addressed. Rather than having a separate whole-school change intervention for different health outcomes, a better approach would likely involve addressing health holistically and motivating delivery in terms of educational and not just health impacts. School leaders do not need to wait for changes in education policies to use such interventions to achieve benefits for student health and education. However, more supportive policy would certainly help, and this is the subject of the next chapter.

9

Detoxifying education policy

Introduction

The pandemic resulted in long school closures worldwide, the duration of which varied between countries, affecting 1.6 billion learners.[252] In England, schools were closed for 17 weeks across two lockdowns.[164] School closures harmed student attainment as well as mental health and wellbeing.[161,253–256] Effects were very variable across groups and countries.[255,257] Harms to wellbeing particularly affected girls, disadvantaged and unsupported students, young children and older adolescents.[255,258] Harms to attainment particularly affected disadvantaged students, who generally experienced worse online learning.[160,164,259]

Post pandemic, schools face big challenges with attendance, behaviour, engagement, mental health and attainment.[260] The interventions discussed in this book should help schools manage these challenges. Schools can use the approaches outlined in previous chapters without waiting for government policies to change.

The interventions described don't need schools to be any less focused on student attainment, and in fact some of the approaches have been shown to boost attainment. But a more supportive policy context would help schools to achieve more dramatic improvements. How should education policy change to support such work and make it easier for schools to disrupt the three toxic mechanisms of educational disengagement, lack of school belonging, and student fear and anxiety?

How policy should not change

I should be clear first of all what I am not calling for. I am not calling for a return to academic selection or for the introduction of different schools for different sorts of student. Comprehensive schools are likely to achieve the best overall results. There is some evidence that selective schools marginally benefit their students,[261] but this needs to be weighed against their effect on reducing attainment and increasing inequality among the wider local student population.[262] It is crucial that comprehensive schools attract the middle classes. The 1997–2010 Labour government recognised that this helps ensure middle-class support for taxation to pay for decent public services. It also helps ensure that assertive middle-class parents contribute to demanding the best of local schools. In social policy, it has long been said that a service for the poor can quickly become a poor service.[263] The presence of a broad range of students of all abilities helps ensure that student norms tend towards promoting school engagement.

I am also not arguing for the removal of school autonomy, national curricula, inspections, tracking progress or even league tables. This is despite the fact that the set of changes that have occurred in the last few decades have not produced overall improvements in student attainment. In fact, as mentioned in Chapter 4, there is evidence of a decline in student attainment across OECD countries, which accelerated during the pandemic.[264] There had been a gradual improvement but then a decline from 2012 for reading, a steepening decline for mathematics and an improvement but then a decline from 2009 for science.[170] The UK trend between 2000 and 2023 has been a gradual improvement in reading, a slight decline in mathematics and a more steep decline in science.[170]

This might suggest that the raft of changes in the UK, such as national curricula, inspections, tracking progress and accountability, are not effective or may even be harmful. However, it is not that simple. There is consistent evidence that introducing school autonomy, management and accountability can help improve academic attainment and progress.[152,153,155–158,168] Countries that have reduced accountability have experienced worse trends in attainment.[163] There is more mixed evidence regarding whether competition between schools is associated with higher attainment.[158] For example, as mentioned in Chapter 4, the abolition of league tables in Wales in 2001 resulted in a significant decline in educational attainment.[163] This suggests that merely removing these features in the absence of more effective changes to education policy will simply make things even worse. There may be unintended consequences of particular targets, but it is better to refine and manage these rather than abandon targets altogether.[165] For example, as described in Chapter 4, the original threshold measure of attainment reduced attainment among the least able students because resources were focused on helping 'key marginal' students on the cusp of achieving the threshold.[150] However, the answer was to reform the metric rather than abandon the accountability framework altogether.

How policy should change

My overall argument here is that the accountability system has been very effective in incentivising schools to achieve certain outputs and outcomes; it's just that the outputs and outcomes in question are often the wrong ones. So how should education policy change so that schools generate the right outputs and outcomes and disrupt the toxic mechanisms described in this book?

Pastoral activities and belonging

Schools should be encouraged and enabled to focus much more on building belonging and community. This has been the main focus of interventions described in earlier chapters. Schools should not just be battery farms for individual attainment. Pastoral activities bind students to the school and improve relationships between and among staff and students. Sports, beyond their important role in promoting physical activity and mental health, are valuable for building belonging. Evidence from Germany suggests that boys are more likely to be physically active when their school has a swimming pool and girls when their school has a football pitch.[142] This suggests schools can make a difference to students' physical activity when they offer activities that students might not otherwise try. Communal arts and creativity are similarly valuable for building a school community and promoting mental health, as well as providing skilled entrants into the creative economy. And arts in schools improve attainment.[149]

Schools should also be encouraged to promote student participation and democracy. Research indicates that schools that seek feedback from students have better attainment.[158] As discussed in Chapter 6, students best learn to manage emotions and relationships not by studying this in an abstract way in the classroom, but by negotiating and interacting with each other and with staff as part of normal school activities. So how should government policy encourage these things? Government should give a more prominent place in the national curriculum to sports, arts and citizenship education through participation. Schools should receive additional funding for such activities. Inspectors should give more prominence to these aspects of school life in their reports.

Admissions

School communities should be more diverse in terms of socioeconomic status. Distance to school is an important aspect of selection for most secondary schools in the UK. Proximity to a good school inflates local house prices.[265] In this context, the increase in parental choice has led to more separation of students according to high and low socioeconomic status.[153] Outcomes are generally better for students in schools with more advantaged students.[130] Concentrating disadvantaged students together is likely to amplify underachievement.[183] But wellbeing and engagement in risk behaviours among disadvantaged students are worse when such students comprise only a small minority in schools dominated by more socioeconomically advantaged students.[117,266] This resonates with the findings from qualitative research reported in Chapter 2 about the 'hyper girls' who were students of low socioeconomic status in a schools otherwise dominated by students from families of higher socioeconomic status.[11] Being such a small minority encouraged these students to adopt a siege mentality and actively reject the dominant attainment-focused culture in the school. So what should government do? Schools should be forced to diversify their intakes by increasing the size of their catchment areas and, where there is oversubscription, introducing some element of chance into the admissions process. School lotteries are a common means of determining admissions in high-performing schools in some countries, including New Zealand, Sweden and the US.[267] Furthermore, in England, the funding from the 'pupil premium', which goes to schools in proportion to their intake of disadvantaged students, should be substantially uplifted.

National curriculum

The national curriculum should be broadened. Narrowing the curriculum so that it is overwhelmingly academic was a major policy error. It makes no sense because students have different interests and ambitions, and the economy has a need for diverse skills. Schools need to look at each student and work out how the school can help that student realise their potential. Too often, the focus is instead on how the student can help the school meet its performance targets. For some students, learning traditional academic subjects might be best. For some students, learning vocational skills might be best. For some students, learning academic skills but through vocationally focused project work might be best. This can happen within the same school and with students having the flexibility to change tracks where they want to. A broader curriculum would help ensure all students feel that in going to school, they are learning important skills and are feeling a sense of accomplishment in a valued area. This would help young people develop pro-school markers of identity, status and transition to adulthood.

A recent House of Lords report on secondary schools issued similar recommendations. It makes the point that the current narrowly academic and content-heavy curriculum will not prepare students for future employment:

> Today's 11-year-olds will leave school in the 2030s. They need change to be made urgently. While it is difficult to predict what jobs will be available when they enter the workforce, digital, creative and technical skills are likely to be in even greater demand. Skills such as collaboration, creativity and problem solving are also expected to become increasingly important. Opportunities to develop these skills have, however, been squeezed out of the 11–16 phase. (p 3)[148]

A recent report by the National Foundation for Educational Research identified six key employment skills predicted to be most sought by employers by 2035: communication; collaboration; problem-solving; organising, planning and prioritising work; creative thinking; and information literacy.[268] These should be taken into account in the national curriculum.

School leavers in England today perform worse than those in other countries and worse than previous English cohorts in terms of employability skills.[164] This likely reflects the current content-heavy curriculum and emphasis on rote learning and cramming in teaching methods,[148] which mean skills are not learnt and knowledge is not sustained. The Lords review into secondary education heard evidence that academies are using the greater flexibility they have regarding the curriculum to abandon subjects such as art and design and music.[148] Government policy should broaden the curriculum and, relatedly, the metrics on which schools are held accountable. This would reverse the narrowing that occurred from 2010. The content load of each subject also needs to be reduced so that teaching can use more effective methods and focus on skills, not just rote learning. An education system can have strong performance accountability for schools while also having a broad national curriculum that includes vocational and practical subjects – this was the case under the 1997–2010 Labour government.

Performance metrics

Alongside a broadening of the curriculum, there should be a broadening of performance metrics. The focus on the EBacc subjects in some of the key performance metrics for schools has encouraged schools to narrow their curricula and reduce vocational subjects and arts and sports activities. There has been a consequent decline in take-up of these subjects.[148,269] The key metric for schools should focus on progress, not absolute attainment. It would be perfectly possible for a progress metric for secondary schools to encompass attainment at age 16 across academic and vocational subjects while adjusting for academic attainment at the end of primary school. There should also be a new performance metric based on a measure of student sense of belonging and connection in school, derived from regular online surveys of students.

Effective pedagogy

Pedagogy needs to be improved by basing it on evidence from randomised controlled trials. The OECD's Programme for International Student Assessment (PISA) is extremely influential. Education ministries in different countries care deeply where their country ranks in this assessment, and there are frequent exhortations to adopt the pedagogic methods used in the highest-ranking countries.[270] PISA is a useful guide to whether a national school system is performing well overall. However, such country comparisons are not a good guide to what specific pedagogical methods to use. No one would use cross-country comparisons of health systems and outcomes to determine the effectiveness of specific medical interventions. It makes no more sense to do so for pedagogical interventions. What works will be different in different contexts. So we need to make much more use of randomised controlled trials to assess the effectiveness of specific pedagogical approaches. In education policy, we need to move towards 'piecemeal social engineering' based on evidence of effectiveness rather than having regular, massive system changes based on flimsy evidence.[271] The number of trials of pedagogical interventions has hugely increased in recent years, not least due to the leadership and funding provided by the Education Endowment Foundation. This needs to continue, but there needs to be a parallel effort to get all this evidence into practice.

Teachers rarely use evidence of effectiveness when designing their teaching; they rely much more on their own or their colleagues' experience.[272,273] One study of schools in Wales found that 30 per cent of teaching practices had some evidence of effectiveness, 67 per cent had no evidence and 3 per cent had evidence of ineffectiveness.[274] A study in 2019 found no increase in teaching practices being based on evidence over the course of five years.[272] This lack of use of evidence seems to reflect some scepticism about, and antipathy to, evidence-based practice among teachers. This is often rooted in a belief that teaching is more an art than a science. This might partly reflect the fact that schools are bombarded with interventions that spuriously purport to be based on evidence but aren't informed by rigorous evaluation in real-life classrooms. This would include initiatives rooted in lab science, such as cognitive neuroscience, which have not been evaluated in schools.

While scepticism about such interventions is justifiable, broader antipathy to evidence-based practice is misplaced. It is sometimes said that every school or every classroom is different, so it is not possible to apply in one's own school or classroom approaches found to be effective elsewhere. But this argument would imply that teachers can learn nothing from any experience other than their own immediate experience, which is obviously absurd. What is needed is more, not less, evaluation and for evaluations to assess not merely what works but what works for whom under what circumstances. There will always be a role for teacher judgement in determining what interventions should be applied in what circumstances, but this should be informed by a sophisticated evidence base.

In this context of a lack of use of evidence as well as challenging targets, it is perhaps natural that schools turn to instructional practices focused on didactic methods, rote learning and cramming, as reported to the House of Lords inquiry into secondary education.[148] While understandable, this is counterproductive given the strong and consistent evidence that pedagogy is actually more effective when students learn actively and collectively.[149] The Education Endowment Foundation judges different pedagogic approaches according to the number of months they accelerate learning by. Arts participation adds three months of progress. Collaborative learning adds five months. Peer tutoring adds five months. Small group tuition adds four months. In contrast, setting and streaming adds zero months.[149] The use of evidence-based effective pedagogy would help disrupt the toxic mechanism of educational disengagement.

The teaching profession

Recruitment and retention

We need to recruit and retain the best teachers. The UK has high-quality teachers but teacher quality could be even higher.[275] After a period of improvement, the calibre of entrants to teaching has flatlined since 2015, and there is a recruitment crisis in some subjects.[276,277] A significant proportion of secondary school teachers do not have an undergraduate degree in the subject they teach.[278] Teachers vary in effectiveness;[279] effectiveness increases with experience[275,280] but there is increasing staff turnover and exit. The most disadvantaged schools have the least effective teachers.

In the 10 per cent most disadvantaged schools in England (based on the proportion of students eligible for school meals), around a quarter of schools did not meet the Ofsted standard for good teaching, whereas in the 10 per cent least disadvantaged schools, almost all met this standard.[164]

We therefore need to recruit and retain the best teachers. This is likely to be partly down to salaries.[281] The UK spends more on schooling per student than the average across OECD countries (including Finland and Japan). In the UK, headteacher earnings (relative to other graduate professions) are above the OECD average. However, classroom teachers' earnings are below the OECD average.[159] So the government might boost teacher recruitment, the calibre of entrants and teacher retention by improving classroom teachers' salaries. This might be conditional on higher expectations about the quality of new entrants.[275] Singapore recruits entrants to teacher training colleges from the top third of school attainers by offering an attractive study package and working conditions. Some countries, such as Finland, Japan and South Korea, require applicants to pass a competitive exam to become teachers.[275]

However, salaries are not the sole determinant of recruitment and retention. Although trends and prevalence are broadly similar to other occupational groups,[282] teachers' mental health has declined in recent years[283] and teachers enjoy little sense of control over their work or high professional status. Teachers in the UK have very high classroom contact time and insufficient time for preparation. The level of funding of a school is a key determinant of its students' attainment.[284] More funding for schools specifically so that they can reduce contact time and allow more preparation would be very likely to improve teacher retention and also improve the quality of lesson planning.

Training

Teachers' performance can also be improved by their ongoing professional development,[280] but this is currently very variable in its focus and quality.[285] Training teachers in the use of more effective pedagogy can improve attainment.[286] Continuing professional development for teachers should be more tightly controlled so that it focuses on supporting evidence-based practice. Schools should then audit whether practice aligns with effective approaches. Audit involves a cycle of: agreeing what the standard of practice should be, based on evidence of effectiveness; assessing what current practice is; and then agreeing what changes are needed to ensure practice is improved.[287] This would build on existing work. Headteacher observation and performance management as well as peer assessment have been shown to improve the quality of teaching.[169,288] This would be facilitated by an expansion of the non-contact time that teachers have so that they have time for such work. Inspections should assess whether schools are undertaking such audits.

Professional status

But above all else, to recruit and retain the best teachers, the status of teaching as a profession needs to be enhanced. It is often said that the status of teachers is low in the UK compared to countries such as Finland and Singapore. Increased pay and higher calibre of entrants would help, but there is also a need to promote the intellectual autonomy of the teaching profession. As a profession, teachers have little say in what pedagogical approaches are used in schools. Teachers usually appear to be the object rather than the originators of new developments in schooling. Evaluation of pedagogy is largely led by psychologists, economists and social scientists. Approaches are recommended by outside bodies, such as the Educational Endowment Foundation, or imposed by government.

The answer is not a return to the days of individual professional autonomy, when individual teachers were largely unaccountable and could choose pedagogy based on their professional judgement. Sometimes they made good choices but often they made bad choices, as would any professionals left to their own devices. The answer is for teachers, like the medical profession, to take on leadership of evidence-based practice and the research on which this is based. This could be promoted by funders, such as the Educational Endowment Foundation, diverting some of their existing funding to provide research training fellowships for teachers and more funding for implementation science examining how evidence-based approaches are best delivered in practice. Alongside the changes to recruitment, salary and contact time described earlier, this could contribute to a transformation of the professional status of teachers.

Conclusion

This book has described interventions to help schools disrupt the toxic mechanisms of educational disengagement, lack of school belonging, and fear and anxiety. Schools can use such interventions to promote student health and attainment without waiting for government policies to change. But a more supportive policy context would help achieve more dramatic improvements. This does not require the wholesale abandonment of the school autonomy and accountability framework that has dominated policy over the last four decades. This has been effective in incentivising schools to achieve certain outputs and outcomes. However, the outputs and outcomes that have been achieved have often been the wrong ones. Education policy change could help schools generate the right outputs and outcomes and disrupt the toxic mechanisms described in this book. Schools should be encouraged and enabled to focus much more on building belonging and community – for example, by policy placing more emphasis on sports, arts and citizenship. School communities should be rendered more diverse in terms of socioeconomic status, via more use of lotteries in admissions processes, for example. The national curriculum should be broadened so that it includes vocational learning and meets the needs of all, not just the most academic, students. Alongside a broadening of the curriculum, there should be a broadening of performance metrics. Pedagogy needs to be improved by basing it on evidence from randomised controlled trials. The recruitment, retention and continuing professional development of classroom teachers needs to be improved – for example, via better salaries and ongoing training that is more focused on evidence-based pedagogy.

10
Conclusion: detoxifying education

The current generation of young people is less mentally healthy than previous generations. Rates of bullying and other forms of violence remain at worrying high levels in the UK and elsewhere. Use of alcohol, tobacco and other substances has seen recent decline in high-income countries, including the UK. However, there is evidence that this is now levelling off and, for some substances, increasing again. Young people's sexual health is improving globally, but in the UK young people report high levels of risk behaviours and adverse sexual health outcomes. Young people, particularly in high-income countries, tend to have poor diets and engage in insufficient physical activity, with increasing rates of obesity.

Schools are not the only cause of these problems, but they do play an important role. Drawing on qualitative research, I have described the ways in which schools can harm young people's health through mechanisms involving educational disengagement, lack of belonging in school community, and fear and anxiety. Statistical evidence from different kinds of study supports the view that schools have an impact on risk behaviours and health outcomes via these mechanisms. The best evidence is from longitudinal studies that track students over time and examine statistical associations between various school-level characteristics and students' health outcomes or risk behaviours, adjusting for potential confounders. These studies suggest that within education systems, some schools do a better job than others of protecting their students and avoiding the three toxic mechanisms.

Education policy in the last four decades has come to emphasise school autonomy and accountability. There is strong evidence that certain aspects of these developments have brought some benefits in terms of school management efficiency, consistency of standards and student attainment. However, other aspects of these changes have contributed to the toxic mechanisms of educational disengagement, lack of school belonging, and fear and anxiety. In particular, there has been a narrowing of the curriculum to focus on academic subjects and a downgrading of vocational learning as well as arts and sports. There has also been a reversion to regressive and ineffective pedagogies that focus on rote learning and neglect skills. There has been an erosion of collective experiences in schools, which as well as arts and sports activities include assemblies and student participation in decision-making. There has been an increasing use of cruel and ineffective disciplinary methods, which have failed to protect students from violence and disorder. There has also been insufficient support for students coping with the pressures of schoolwork. Therefore, despite some positive developments, something is wrong with schools and our education system.

In recent years, a great many physical and mental health interventions have started to be delivered in schools. These are add-ons, done over and above schools' core mission of educating students. Some, such as classroom health education and mindfulness, are universal and preventative, while others, such as cognitive behavioural therapy and group work, target students already engaging in risk behaviours or with particular physical or mental health problems. Some of these add-on interventions are effective, but many are ineffective and some are harmful. Even when such interventions are effective, schools may lack the motivation, time, capacity or resources to deliver these health interventions with the fidelity needed to ensure they are effective. Teachers often lack the specialist skills needed to take on a health promotion role in schools. While there is certainly a role for some effective school health interventions, they are not a panacea and do not disrupt, but merely compensate for, the toxic mechanisms of school disengagement, lack of school belonging, and fear and anxiety described in this book. On their own, these sorts of sticking plaster interventions are not going to detoxify schools.

There is another way. There is good academic theory and an evidence base for promoting health in schools not via add-on health interventions but via transforming school environments to disrupt the toxic mechanisms to make schools genuinely health-promoting institutions. Chapter 6 describes the theoretical basis for the Learning Together intervention as well as evidence from its process and outcome evaluation. These evaluations found that the intervention was feasible and acceptable to deliver and that it benefited students – for example, in terms of reduced bullying, reduced substance use, improved mental health and improved educational attainment.

Furthermore, Learning Together is not an isolated example of an intervention that improves young people's health by transforming school environments. It was strongly informed by the Aban Aya and Gatehouse interventions, conducted in US middle schools and Australian secondary schools, respectively. These in turn were influenced by the Seattle Social Development Project delivered in US elementary schools. An array of school transformation interventions have now been evaluated across settings spanning Africa, Asia, Europe, North America and Oceania. These have benefited students in terms of reduced violence and substance use, improved mental health, physical activity and sexual health as well as higher educational attainment. A systematic review of the effects of school-based interventions that promote student commitment to school via transforming schools' core business found that these tended to reduce both violence and substance use in the short and the long term.

These sorts of intervention offer a flexible and sustainable way for schools to promote health without needing lots of lesson time or requiring teachers to develop new skill sets. Such interventions aim to transform how schools are run in order to disrupt the toxic mechanisms described in this book, rather than merely attempting to compensate for such toxic mechanisms. These interventions are flexible, and school leaders will need to take different approaches depending on their students' needs and the capacity within their school and the wider country. Rather than having a separate whole-school change intervention for different health outcomes, a better approach would be to address health holistically and motivate delivery through focusing on educational and not just health impacts.

School leaders do not need to wait for changes in education policies to use such interventions to achieve benefits for student health, and indeed the interventions recommended in this book should help schools meet their education targets. However, more supportive education policy would certainly help. This should not involve the wholesale abandonment of the school autonomy and accountability framework that has dominated policy over the last four decades. This framework has been effective in incentivising schools to achieve certain outputs and outcomes. The problem is that the outputs and outcomes that have been achieved were often the wrong ones. Education policy should be tweaked, not revolutionised, in order to enable schools to generate the right outputs and outcomes and disrupt the toxic mechanisms described in this book.

Schools should focus much more on building belonging and community, supported by policy placing more emphasis on sports, arts and citizenship. School communities should be diversified in terms of students' socioeconomic status, via more use of lotteries in admissions processes, for example. National curricula should be broadened to include vocational learning and meet the needs of all, not just the most academic, students. Broadening the curriculum should be accompanied by broadening the performance metrics. Classroom pedagogy needs to be improved by basing it on evidence from randomised controlled trials. The recruitment, retention and continuing professional development of classroom teachers needs to be improved – for example, via better salaries and ongoing training that is more focused on evidence-based pedagogy.

Schools have the potential to enormously benefit the health and wellbeing of young people. Remaining in school throughout adolescence is a key global driver of better health among adolescents as well as later parenthood and lower mortality and better health, social and economic outcomes in adulthood. Being in school can promote health by broadening life choices, improving incomes and protecting young people from exploitation. Across the world, school enrolments are rising but many young people still miss out on the full benefits schooling can bring. The key argument made in this book is that although the quantity of education, in the form of enrolments and years of schooling, matters for health, so too does the quality of schooling that young people receive. Schools and education systems can be transformed so that they maximise the benefits of education while avoiding the toxic mechanisms of educational disengagement, lack of school belonging, and fear and anxiety, which currently damage the lives of so many young people.

References

1. Commission on Social Determinants of Health. *Closing the Gap in a Generation: Health Equity through Action on the Social Determinants of Health*. Geneva: World Health Organization, 2008.
2. IHME-CHAIN Collaborators. Effects of education on adult mortality: a global systematic review and meta-analysis. *The Lancet Public Health*, 2024, 9(3): e155–e165.
3. Viner RM, Hargreaves DS, Ward J et al. The health benefits of secondary education in adolescents and young adults: an international analysis in 186 low-, middle- and high-income countries from 1990 to 2013. *Social Science & Medicine Population Health*, 2017, 3: 162–71.
4. UNESCO. *New Estimation Confirms Out-of-School Population is Growing in Sub-Saharan Africa*. Montreal: UNESCO Institute for Statistics, 2022.
5. Paulle B. *Toxic Schools*. Chicago, IL: University of Chicago Press, 2013.
6. Bonell C, Warren E, Melendez-Torres GJ. Methodological reflections on using qualitative research to explore the causal mechanisms of complex health interventions. *Evaluation*, 2022, 28(2): 166–81.
7. Blakemore SJ. Avoiding social risk in adolescence. *Current Directions in Psychological Science*, 2018, 27(2): 116–22.
8. Erikson EH. *Identity: Youth and Crisis*. New York: Norton, 1968.
9. Benjamin S. *The Micropolitics of Inclusive Education: An Ethnography*. Buckingham: Open University Press, 2002.
10. Bonell C, Blakemore SJ, Fletcher A et al. Role theory of schools and adolescent health. *The Lancet Child and Adolescent Health*, 2019, 3(10): 742–8.
11. Fletcher A, Bonell C, Rhodes T. New counter-school cultures: female students' drug use at a high-achieving secondary school. *British Journal of Sociology of Education*, 2009, 30(5): 549–62.
12. Reay D. *Miseducation*. Bristol: Policy Press, 2017.
13. Dance J. *Tough Fronts: The Impact of Street Culture on Schooling*. New York: Routledge/Farmer, 2002.
14. Willis P. *Learning to Labour: How Working Class Kids Get Working Class Jobs*. Aldershot: Saxon House, 1977.
15. Anderson E. *Code of the Street: Decency, Violence, and the Moral Life of the Inner City*. New York: Norton, 1999.
16. Milner M. *Freaks, Geeks and Cool Kids*. London: Routledge, 2006.
17. Henderson S, Holland J, McGrellis S et al. *Inventing Adulthoods: A Biographical Approach to Youth Transitions*. London: Sage, 2007.
18. Measham F. 'Doing gender' – 'doing drugs': conceptualizing the gendering of drug cultures. *Contemporary Drug Problems*, 2002, 29(2): 335–73.
19. Furlong A, Cartmel F. *Young People and Social Change: New Perspectives*. Milton Keynes: Open University Press, 2007.

20. Arai L. Low expectations, sexual attitudes and knowledge: explaining teenage pregnancy and fertility in English communities. Insights from qualitative research, *The Sociological Review*, 2003, 51(2): 199–217.
21. Jamal F, Fletcher A, Harden A et al. The school environment and student health: a systematic review and meta-ethnography of qualitative research. *BMC Public Health*, 2013, 13(1): art 798. doi: 10.1186/1471-2458-13-798
22. Bonell C, Fletcher A, Sorhaindo A et al. How market-oriented education policies might influence young people's health: development of a logic model from qualitative case studies in English secondary schools. *Journal of Epidemiology and Community Health*, 2012, 66(7): art e24. doi: 10.1136/jech.2011.137539
23. Peterson AJ, Bonell C. School experiences and young women's pregnancy and parenthood decisions: a systematic review and synthesis of qualitative research. *Health and Place*, 2018, 53: 52–61.
24. Davidson E. Responsible girls: the spatialized politics of feminine success and aspiration in a divided Silicon Valley, USA. *Gender, Place and Culture*, 2015, 22(3): 390–404.
25. Putnam RD. *Bowling Alone: The Collapse and Revival of American Community*. New York: Simon & Schuster, 2000.
26. Ogbu JU. *Black American Students in an Affluent Suburb: A Study of Academic Disengagement*. Mahwah, NJ: Lawrence Erlbaum Associates, 2003.
27. Holt-Lunstad J, Robles TF, Sbarra DA. Advancing social connection as a public health priority in the United States. *American Psychologist*, 2017, 72(6): 517–30.
28. Sebastian C, Viding E, Williams KD et al. Social brain development and the affective consequences of ostracism in adolescence. *Brain and Cognition*, 2010, 72(1): 134–45.
29. Fletcher A, Bonell C, Sorhaindo A et al. Cannabis use and 'safe' identities in an inner-city school risk environment. *International Journal of Drug Policy*, 2009, 20(3): 244–50.
30. Brooks F, Klemera E, Chester K et al. *HBSC England National Report: Findings from the 2018 HBSC Study for England*. Hatfield: University of Hertfordshire, 2020.
31. Fletcher A, Bonell C, Sorhaindo A et al. How might schools influence young people's drug use? Development of theory from qualitative case-study research. *Journal of Adolescent Health*, 2009, 45(2): 126–32.
32. Jamal F, Bonell C, Harden A et al. The social ecology of girls' bullying practices: exploratory research in two London schools. *Sociology of Health & Illness*, 2015, 37(5): 731–44.
33. Astor RA, Meyer HA, Behre WJ. Unowned places and times: maps and interviews about violence in high schools. *American Educational Research Journal*, 1999, 36(1): 3–42.

34. Haselswerdt MV, Lenhardt AMC. Reframing school violence: listening to voices of students. *Educational Forum*, 2003, 67(4): 326–36.
35. Palmer S. *Toxic Childhood: How the Modern World Is Damaging Our Children and What We Can Do about It*. London: Orion Publishing, 2006.
36. Roome T, Soan C. GCSE exam stress: student perceptions of the effects on wellbeing and performance. *Pastoral Care in Education*, 2019, 37(4): 297–315.
37. Cousins LH. Toward a sociocultural context for understanding violence and disruption in black urban schools and communities. *Journal of Sociology & Social Welfare*, 1997, 24(2): art 4. doi: 10.15453/0191-5096.2415
38. Evans R, Hurrell C. The role of schools in children and young people's self-harm and suicide: systematic review and meta-ethnography of qualitative research. *BMC Public Health*, 2016, 16(1): art 401. doi: 10.1186/s12889-016-3065-2
39. Brunson RK, Miller JM. Schools, neighborhoods, and adolescent conflicts: a situational examination of reciprocal dynamics. *Justice Quarterly*, 2009, 26(2): 183–210.
40. Wills W, Backett-Milburn K, Gregory S et al. The influence of the secondary school setting on the food practices of young teenagers from disadvantaged backgrounds in Scotland. *Health Education Research*, 2005, 20(4): 458–65.
41. Pike J, Colquhoun D. The relationship between policy and place: the role of school meals in addressing health inequalities. *Health Sociology Review*, 2009, 18(1): 50–60.
42. Solmi M, Radua J, Olivola M et al. Age at onset of mental disorders worldwide: large-scale meta-analysis of 192 epidemiological studies. *Molecular Psychiatry*, 2022, 27(1): 281–95.
43. Pitchforth J, Fahy K, Ford T et al. Mental health and well-being trends among children and young people in the UK, 1995–2014: analysis of repeated cross-sectional national health surveys. *Psychological Medicine*, 2019, 49(8): 1275–85.
44. Collishaw S. Annual research review: secular trends in child and adolescent mental health. *Journal of Child Psychology and Psychiatry*, 2015, 56(3): 370–93.
45. Lessof C, Ross A, Brind R et al. *Longitudinal Study of Young People in England Cohort 2: Health and Wellbeing at Wave 2*. London: Department for Education, 2016.
46. Twenge J, Cooper A, Joiner T et al. Age, period, and cohort trends in mood disorder indicators and suicide-related outcomes in a nationally representative dataset, 2005–2017. *Journal of Abnormal Psychology*, 2019, 128(3): 185–19.

47. Collishaw S, Sellers R. Trends in child and adolescent mental health prevalence, outcomes, and inequalities. In Taylor E, Verhulst F, Wong J et al (eds) *Mental Health and Illness of Children and Adolescents Mental Health and Illness Worldwide*. Singapore: Springer, 2020, pp 1–11.
48. Bor W, Dean AJ, Najman J et al. Are child and adolescent mental health problems increasing in the 21st century? A systematic review. *Australian & New Zealand Journal of Psychiatry*, 2014, 48(7): 606–16.
49. Orben A. Teenagers, screens and social media: a narrative review of reviews and key studies. *Social Psychiatry and Psychiatric Epidemiology*, 2020, 55(4): 407–4.
50. Orben A, Przybylski AK, Blakemore SJ et al. Windows of developmental sensitivity to social media. *Nature Communication*, 2022, 13(1): art 1649. doi: 10.1038/s41467-022-29296-3
51. Jerrim J. The mental health of adolescents in England: how does it vary during their time at school? *British Educational Research Journal*, 2021, 48(2): 330–53.
52. Wright B, Garside M, Allgar V et al. A large population-based study of the mental health and wellbeing of children and young people in the north of England. *Clinical Child Psychology and Psychiatry*, 2020, 25(4): 877–90.
53. Public Health England. *Measuring Mental Wellbeing in Children and Young People*, 2015. Available at: https://assets.publishing.service.gov.uk/media/5c2f66daed915d731281fdc2/Measuring_mental_wellbeing_in_children_and_young_people.pdf (Accessed 3 November 2020).
54. Collishaw S, Furzer E, Thapar AK et al. Brief report: a comparison of child mental health inequalities in three UK population cohorts. *European Child and Adolescent Psychiatry*, 2019, 28(11): 1547–49.
55. Ahmad G, McManus S, Bécares L et al. Explaining ethnic variations in adolescent mental health: a secondary analysis of the Millennium Cohort Study. *Social Psychiatry and Psychiatric Epidemiology*, 2022, 57(4): 817–28.
56. Clayborne Z, Varin M, Colman I. Systematic review and meta-analysis: adolescent depression and long-term psychosocial outcomes. *Journal of the American Academy of Child & Adolescent Psychiatry*, 2019, 58(1): 72–9.
57. Finning K, Ukoumunne OC, Ford T et al. The association between child and adolescent depression and poor attendance at school: a systematic review and meta-analysis. *Journal of Affective Disorders*, 2019, 245: 928–38.
58. Finning K, Ukoumunne OC, Ford T et al. The association between anxiety and poor attendance at school – a systematic review. *Child and Adolescent Mental Health*, 2019, 24(3): 205–16.
59. Fergusson D, Woodward L. Mental health, educational, and social role outcomes of adolescents with depression. *Archives of General Psychiatry*, 2002, 59(3): 225–31.

60. Gutman LM, Vorhaus J. *The Impact of Pupil Behaviour and Wellbeing on Educational Outcomes*. London: Department for Education, 2012.
61. Bücker S, Nuraydin S, Simonsmeier BA et al. Subjective well-being and academic achievement: a meta-analysis. *Journal of Research in Personality*, 2018, 74: 83–94.
62. Smith L, López Sánchez GF, Haro JM et al. Temporal trends in bullying victimization among adolescents aged 12–15 years from 29 countries: a global perspective. *Journal of Adolescent Health*, 2023, 73(3): 582–90.
63. Molcho M, Craig W, Due P et al. Cross-national time trends in bullying behaviour 1994–2006: findings from Europe and North America. *International Journal of Public Health*, 2009, 54(supp 2): S225–S234.
64. Department for Education. *National Behaviour Survey: Findings from Academic Year 2021/22*. London: Department for Education, 2023.
65. Arseneault L. Annual research review: the persistent and pervasive impact of being bullied in childhood and adolescence: implications for policy and practice. *Journal of Child Psychology and Psychiatry*, 2017, 59(4): 405–21.
66. Wincentak K, Connolly J, Card N. Teen dating violence: a meta-analytic review of prevalence rates. *Psychology of Violence*, 2017, 7(2): 224–41.
67. Leen E, Sorbring E, Mawer M et al. Prevalence, dynamic risk factors and the efficacy of primary interventions for adolescent dating violence: an international review. *Aggression and Violent Behavior*, 2013, 18(1): 159–74.
68. Marcantonio TL, Weese J, Willis M. Rates of forced sexual experiences among high school students from 2001 to 2019. *Journal of Interpersonal Violence*, 2022, 37(21–22): art NP21045-NP21069. doi 10.1177/08862605211055155
69. Vashishtha R, Pennay A, Dietze P et al. Trends in adolescent drinking across 39 high-income countries: exploring the timing and magnitude of decline. *European Journal of Public Health*, 2021, 31(2): 424–31.
70. Pape H, Rossow I, Brunborg GS. Adolescents drink less: how, who and why? A review of the recent research literature. *Drug and Alcohol Review*, 2018, 37(supp 1): S98–S114.
71. NHS Digital. *Smoking, Drinking and Drug Use among Young People in England, 2021*. London: NHS Digital, 2022.
72. Charrier L, van Dorsselaer S, Canale N et al. *A Focus on Adolescent Substance Use in Europe, Central Asia and Canada: Health Behaviour in School-Aged Children. International Report from the 2021/2022 Survey Volume 3*. Copenhagen: WHO Regional Office for Europe, 2024.
73. Hewitt G, Anthony R, Moore G et al. *Student Health and Wellbeing In Wales: Report of the 2017/18 Health Behaviour in School-Aged Children Survey and School Health Research Network Student Health and Wellbeing Survey*. Cardiff: Cardiff University, 2019.

74. Loy JK, Seitz NN, Bye EK et al. Trends in alcohol consumption among adolescents in Europe: do changes occur in concert? *Drug and Alcohol Dependence*, 2021, 228: art 109020. doi: 10.1016/j.drugalcdep.2021.109020
75. McKee M. Evidence and e-cigarettes: explaining English exceptionalism. *American Journal of Public Health*, 2019, 109(7): 965–6.
76. Glasser A, Abudayyeh H, Cantrell J et al. Patterns of e-cigarette use among youth and young adults: review of the impact of e-cigarettes on cigarette smoking. *Nicotine Tobacco Research*, 2019, 21(10): 1320–30.
77. Hallingberg B, Maynard OM, Bauld L et al. Have e-cigarettes renormalised or displaced youth smoking? Results of a segmented regression analysis of repeated cross sectional survey data in England, Scotland and Wales. *Tobacco Control*, 2020, 29(2): 207–16.
78. Office for National Statistics. *Smoking, Drinking and Drug Use among Young People in England, 2021*. London: Office for National Statistics, 2022.
79. Liang M, Simelane S, Fortuny Fillo G et al. The state of adolescent sexual and reproductive health. *Journal of Adolescent Health*, 2019, 65: S3–S15.
80. World Bank. Adolescent fertility rate (births per 1,000 women ages 15–19), 2022. Available at: https://data.worldbank.org/indicator/SP.ADO.TFRT
81. Lewis R, Tanton C, Mercer CH et al. Heterosexual practices among young people in Britain: evidence from three national surveys of sexual attitudes and lifestyles. *Journal of Adolescent Health*, 2017, 61(6): 694–702.
82. Palmer MJ, Clarke L, Ploubidis GB et al. Is 'sexual competence' at first heterosexual intercourse associated with subsequent sexual health status? *Journal of Sex Research*, 2017, 54(1): 91–104.
83. Girlguiding. *Girls' Attitudes Survey 2013. What Girls Say about Equality for Girls*. London: Girlguiding, 2014.
84. Kar SK, Choudhury A, Singh AP. Understanding normal development of adolescent sexuality: a bumpy ride. *Journal of Human Reproductive Science*, 2015, 8(2): 70–4.
85. Sweeting H, Blake C, Riddell J et al. Sexual harassment in secondary school: prevalence and ambiguities: a mixed methods study in Scottish schools. *PLoS One*, 2022, 17(2): art e0262248. doi: 10.1371/journal.pone.0262248
86. YouGov. *End Violence Against Women Poll Results*. London: End Violence Against Women, 2010.
87. Witkowska E, Menckel E. Perceptions of sexual harassment in Swedish high schools: experiences and school-environment problems. *European Journal of Public Health*, 2005, 15(1): 78–85.
88. Clear E, Coker A, Cook-Craig P et al. Sexual harassment victimization and perpetration among high school students. *Violence Against Women*, 2014, 20: 1203–19.

89. Hill C, Kearl H. *Crossing the Line: Sexual Harassment at School.* Washington, DC: American Association of University Women, 2011.
90. Attar-Schwartz S. Peer sexual harassment victimization at school: the roles of student characteristics, cultural affiliation, and school factors. *American Journal of Orthopsychiatry*, 2009, 79(3): 407–20.
91. Timmerman G. A comparison between unwanted sexual behavior by teachers and by peers in secondary schools. *Journal of Youth and Adolescence*, 2002, 31(5): 397–404.
92. Lipson J. *Hostile Hallways: Bullying, Teasing, and Sexual Harassment in School.* Washington, DC: American Association of University Women Educational Foundation, 2001.
93. Chiodo D, Wolfe D, Crooks C et al. Impact of sexual harassment victimization by peers on subsequent adolescent victimization and adjustment: a longitudinal study. *Journal of Adolescent Health*, 2009, 45(3): 246–52.
94. Bendixen M, Daveronis J, Kennair LEO. The effects of non-physical peer sexual harassment on high school students' psychological well-being in Norway: consistent and stable findings across studies. *International Journal of Public Health*, 2018, 63(1): 3–11.
95. NCD Risk Factor Collaboration. Worldwide trends in underweight and obesity from 1990 to 2022: a pooled analysis of 3663 population-representative studies with 222 million children, adolescents, and adults. *The Lancet*, 2024, 16(10431): 1027–50.
96. Office for Health Improvement and Disparities. *Patterns and Trends in Child Obesity in England: A Presentation of the Latest Data from the National Child Measurement Programme and Health Survey for England*, 2020. Available at: www.gov.uk/government/publications/child-obesity-patterns-and-trends (Accessed 15 September 2024).
97. Guthold R, Stevens GA, Riley LM et al. Global trends in insufficient physical activity among adolescents: a pooled analysis of 298 population-based surveys with 1.6 million participants. *The Lancet Child and Adolescent Health*, 2020, 4(1): 23–35.
98. Gilmore AB, Fabbri A, Baum F et al. Defining and conceptualising the commercial determinants of health. *The Lancet*, 2023, 401(10383): 1194–213.
99. Ashcraft A, Fernández-Val I, Lang K. The consequences of teenage childbearing: consistent estimates when abortion makes miscarriage non-random. *The Economic Journal*, 2013, 123(571): 875–905.
100. Ermisch J. *Does a 'Teen-Birth' Have Longer-Term Impacts on the Mother? Suggestive Evidence from the British Household Panel Survey.* Colchester: Institute for Social and Economic Research, 2003.

[101] Berthoud R, Ermisch J, Francesconi M et al. *Long-Term Consequences of Teenage Births or Parents and their Children*, Teenage Pregnancy Research Programme Research Briefing No 1. London: Department of Health, 2004.

[102] Francesconi M. Adult outcomes for children of teenage mothers. *Scandinavian Journal of Economics*, 2008, 110(1): 93–117.

[103] Bonell C, Allen E, Strange V et al. The effect of dislike of school on risk of teenage pregnancy: testing of hypotheses using longitudinal data from a randomised trial of sex education. *Journal of Epidemiology and Community Health*, 2005, 59(3): 223–30.

[104] Peterson A, Allen E, Viner R et al. Effects of the school environment on early sexual risk behaviour: a longitudinal analysis of students in English secondary schools. *Journal of Adolescence*, 2020, 85: 106–14.

[105] Sweeting H, West P, Young R et al. Can we explain increases in young people's psychological distress over time? *Social Science & Medicine*, 2010, 71(10): 1819–30.

[106] West P, Sweeting H, Leyland A. School effects on pupils' health behaviours: evidence in support of the health promoting school. *Research Papers in Education*, 2004, 19(3): 261–91.

[107] Kuhn L, Bradshaw S, Donkin A et al. *PISA 2018 Additional Analyses: What Does PISA Tell Us about the Wellbeing of 15-Year-Olds?* Slough: National Foundation for Educational Research, 2021.

[108] Govorova E, Benítez I, Muñiz J. Predicting student well-being: network analysis based on PISA 2018. *International Journal of Environmental Research and Public Health*, 2020, 17(11): art 4014. doi: 10.3390/ijerph17114014

[109] Kidger J, Araya R, Donovan J et al. The effect of the school environment on the emotional health of adolescents: a systematic review. *Pediatrics*, 2012, 129(5): 925–49.

[110] Zhu LA. A multi-level analysis on school connectedness, family support, and adolescent depression: evidence from the National Longitudinal Study of Adolescent Health, 1995–1996. *Social Sciences*, 2018, 7(5): art 72. doi: 10.3390/socsci7050072

[111] Raniti M, Rakesh D, Patton GC et al. The role of school connectedness in the prevention of youth depression and anxiety: a systematic review with youth consultation. *BMC Public Health*, 2022, 22: art 2152. doi: 10.1186/s12889-022-14364-6

[112] Halladay J, MacKillop J, Munn C et al. Individual- and school-level patterns of substance use and mental health symptoms in a population-based sample of secondary students: a multilevel latent profile analysis. *Drug and Alcohol Dependence*, 2022, 240: art 109647. doi: 10.1016/j.drugalcdep.2022.109647

113. Bond L, Butler H, Thomas L et al. Social and school connectedness in early secondary school as predictors of late teenage substance use, mental health, and academic outcomes. *Journal of Adolescent Health*, 2007, 40(4): e9–e18.
114. Rose ID, Lesesne CA, Sun J et al. The relationship of school connectedness to adolescents' engagement in co-occurring health risks: a meta-analytic review. *Journal of School Nursing*, 2024, 40(1): 58–73.
115. Weatherson KA, O'Neill M, Lau EY et al. The protective effects of school connectedness on substance use and physical activity. *Journal of Adolescent Health*, 63(6): 724–31.
116. Shochet IM, Dadds MR, Ham D, Montague R. School connectedness is an underemphasized parameter in adolescent mental health: results of a community prediction study. *Journal of Clinical Child and Adolescent Psychology*, 2006, 35(2): 170–79. doi: 10.1207/s15374424jccp3502_1
117. Moore GF, Littlecott HJ, Evans R et al. School composition, school culture and socioeconomic inequalities in young people's health: multi-level analysis of the Health Behaviour in School-aged Children (HBSC) survey in Wales. *British Educational Research Journal*, 43(2): 310–29.
118. Organisation for Economic Co-operation and Development. *PISA 2018 Results (Volume III): What School Life Means for Students*. Paris: OECD Publishing, 2019. Available at: www.oecd.org/publications/pisa-2018-results-volume-iii-acd78851-en.htm (Accessed 7 January 2021).
119. Cook PJ, Gottfredson DC, Na C. School crime control and prevention. *Crime and Justice*, 2010, 39: 313–440.
120. Ingram J, Stiff J, Cadwallader S et al. *PISA 2022: National Report for England*. London: Department for Education, 2023.
121. Cosma A, Stevens G, Martin G et al. Cross-national time trends in adolescent mental well-being from 2002 to 2018 and the explanatory role of schoolwork pressure. *Journal of Adolescent Health*, 2020, 66: S50–S58.
122. Shackleton N, Hale D, Bonell C et al. Intra-class correlation values for adolescent health outcomes in secondary schools in 21 European countries. *Social Science and Medicine Population Health*, 2016, 2: 217–25.
123. Hale DR, Patalay P, Fitzgerald-Yau N et al. School-level variation in health outcomes in adolescence: analysis of three longitudinal studies in England. *Prevention Science*, 2014, 15(4): 600–10.
124. Sellström E, Bremberg S. Is there a 'school effect' on pupil outcomes? A review of multilevel studies. *Journal of Epidemiology & Community Health*, 2006, 60(2): 149–55.
125. Bonell C, Jamal F, Harden A et al. Systematic review of the effects of schools and school environment interventions on health: evidence mapping and synthesis. *Public Health Research*, 2013, 1(1). doi:10.3310/phr01010

[126] Barker KM, Brown S, Pitpitan EV et al. Adolescent alcohol use: use of social network analysis and cross-classified multilevel modeling to examine peer group, school, and neighborhood-level influences. *American Journal of Drug and Alcohol Abuse*, 2023, 49(5): 576–86.

[127] Maes L, Lievens J. Can the school make a difference? A multilevel analysis of adolescent risk and health behaviour. *Social Science & Medicine*, 2003, 56(3): 517–29.

[128] Govorova E, Benítez I, Muñiz J. How schools affect student well-being: a cross-cultural approach in 35 OECD countries. *Frontiers in Psychology*, 2020, 25(11). doi: 10.3389/fpsyg.2020.00431

[129] Hinze V, Montero-Marin J, Blakemore SJ et al. Student- and school-level factors associated with mental health and well-being in early adolescence. *Journal of the American Academy of Child and Adolescent Psychiatry*, 2024, 63(2): 266–82.

[130] Saab H, Klinger D. School differences in adolescent health and wellbeing: findings from the Canadian Health Behaviour in School-aged Children Study. *Social Science & Medicine*, 2010, 70(6): 850–58.

[131] Ford T, Degli Esposti M, Crane C et al. The role of schools in early adolescents' mental health: findings from the MYRIAD study. *Journal of the American Academy of Child and Adolescent Psychiatry*, 2021, 60(12): 1467–78.

[132] Jakubowski M, Gajderowicz T. Student well-being factors: a multilevel analysis of PISA 2015 international data. *European Research Studies Journal*, 2020, 23(4): 1312–33.

[133] Murray DM, Catellier DJ, Hannan PJ et al. School-level intraclass correlation for physical activity in adolescent girls. *Medicine and Science in Sports and Exercise*, 2004, 36(5): 876–82.

[134] Goodfellow C, Willis M, Inchley J et al. Mental health and loneliness in Scottish schools: a multilevel analysis of data from the health behaviour in school-aged children study. *British Journal of Educational Psychology*, 2023, 93(2): 608–25.

[135] Bonell CP, Parry W, Wells H et al. The effects of the school environment on student health: a systematic review of multi-level studies. *Health and Place*, 2013, 21: 180–91.

[136] White CN, Warner LA. Influence of family and school-level factors on age of sexual initiation. *Journal of Adolescent Health*, 2015, 56(2): 231–7.

[137] Epstein M, Furlong M, Kosterman R et al. Adolescent age of sexual initiation and subsequent adult health outcomes. *American Journal of Public Health*, 2018, 108(6): 822–8.

[138] Bonell C, Beaumont E, Dodd M et al. Effects of school environments on student risk-behaviours: evidence from a longitudinal study of secondary schools in England. *Journal of Epidemiology and Community Health*, 2019, 73: 502–8.

139 Gottfredson DC, DiPietro SM. School size, social capital, and student victimization. *Sociology of Education*, 2011, 84: 69–89.
140 Gendron BP, Williams KR, Guerra NG. An analysis of bullying among students within schools: estimating the effects of individual normative beliefs, self-esteem, and school climate. *Journal of School Violence*, 2011, 10: 160–4.
141 Karvonen S, Vikat A, Rimpelä M. The role of school context in the increase in young people's health complaints in Finland. *Journal of Adolescent Health*, 2005, 28(1): 1–16.
142 Czerwinski F, Finne E, Kolip P et al. Individual and school level correlates of moderate to vigorous physical activity among schoolchildren in Germany – a multi-level analysis. *BMC Public Health*, 2015, 15: art 393. doi: 10.1186/s12889-015-1715-4
143 Rolph C. *Understanding Education Policy*. London: Sage, 2023.
144 Judt T. *Postwar: A History of Europe Since 1945*. London: Penguin, 2005.
145 Callaghan J. 'A rational debate based on the facts', speech delivered at Ruskin college, 18 October. Available at: www.education-uk.org/documents/speeches/1976ruskin.html (Accessed 28 October 2024).
146 Arnott M, Ozga J. Education and nationalism: the discourse of education policy in Scotland. *Discourse: Studies in the Cultural Politics of Education*, 2010, 31: 335–50.
147 Egon D. Devolution, education policy and inspection in Wales: a policy analysis. In Keane A (ed) *Watchdogs or Visionaries? Perspectives on the History of the Education Inspectorate in Wales*. Cardiff: University of Wales Press, 2022.
148 House of Lords. *Requires Improvement: Urgent Change for 11–16 Education: Education for 11–16 Year Olds Committee Report of Session 2023–24*. HL Paper 17. London: House of Lords, 2024.
149 Education Endowment Foundation. Teaching and Learning Toolkit: an accessible summary of education evidence. Available at: https://educationendowmentfoundation.org.uk/education-evidence/teaching-learning-toolkit (Accessed 15 April 2024).
150 Burgess S, Propper C, Slater H et al. *Who Wins and Who Loses from School Accountability? The Distribution of Educational Gain in English Secondary Schools*, CMPO Working Paper Series, No 05/128. Bristol: CMPO, University of Bristol, 2005.
151 Congressional Research Service. *The Elementary and Secondary Education Act (ESEA), as Amended by the Every Student Succeeds Act (ESSA): A Primer*. Washington, DC: US Congress, 2024.
152 Bloom N, Lemos R, Sadun R et al. Does management matter in schools? *Economic Journal*, 2015, 125(584): 647–74.

[153] Bradley S, Taylor J. The effect of the quasi-market on the efficiency-equity trade-off in the secondary school sector. *Bulletin of Economic Research*, 2002, 54: 295–314.

[154] Thomson S, Burgess S. *Beyond the Threshold: The Implications for Pupil Achievement of Reforming school Performance Metrics*, Bristol University Working Paper. Bristol: University of Bristol, 2022.

[155] Dee T, Jacob B. *The Impact of No Child Left Behind on Student Achievement*, NBER Working Paper No 15531. Cambridge, MA: NBER, 2009.

[156] Hanushek EA, Link S, Woessmann L. Does school autonomy make sense everywhere? Panel estimates from PISA. *Journal of Development Economics*, 2013, 104: 212–32.

[157] Organisation for Economic Co-operation and Development. *PISA 2009 Results: What Makes a School Successful? Resources, Policies and Practices, Volume IV*, 2010. Available at: www.oecd.org/pisa/pisaproducts/48852721.pdf (Accessed 12 April 2024).

[158] Organisation for Economic Co-operation and Development. *PISA 2018 Results (Volume V): Effective Policies, Successful Schools, PISA*. Paris: OECD Publishing, 2020. Available at: https://doi.org/10.1787/ca768d40-en (Accessed 12 April 2024).

[159] Organisation for Economic Co-operation and Development. *Education at a Glance 2023: OECD Indicators*. Paris: OECD Publishing, 2023.

[160] Nelson J, Sharp C. *Schools' Responses to COVID-19: Key Findings from the Wave 1 Survey*. Slough: National Foundation for Educational Research, 2020.

[161] Organisation for Economic Co-operation and Development. *PISA 2022 Results (Volume I): The State of Learning and Equity in Education*. Paris: OECD Publishing, 2023.

[162] Sizmur J, Ager R, Bradshaw J et al. *Achievement of 15-Year-Olds in England: PISA 2018 Results*, 2019. Available at: https://assets.publishing.service.gov.uk/media/5f20292e8fa8f57ac3af2d11/PISA_2018_England_Exec_summary.pdf (Accessed 7 January 2021).

[163] Burgess S, Wilson D, Worth J. A natural experiment in school accountability: the impact of school performance information on pupil progress. *Journal of Public Economics*, 2013, 106: 57–67.

[164] Farquharson C, McNally S, Tahir I. *Educational Inequalities*. London: Institute for Fiscal Studies, 2022.

[165] Barber M. *How to Run a Government*. London: Penguin, 2015.

[166] Clarke M, Haines Lyon C, Walker E et al. The banality of education policy: discipline as extensive evil in the neoliberal era. *Power and Education*, 2021, 13(3): 187–204.

167. Bonell C, Allen E, Warren E et al. Initiating change in the school environment to reduce bullying and aggression: a cluster randomised controlled trial of the Learning Together (LT) intervention in English secondary schools. *The Lancet*, 2018, 392(10163): 2452–64.
168. Hanushek E, Raymond M. Does school accountability lead to improved student performance? *Journal of Policy Analysis and Management*, 2005, 24(2): 297–327.
169. Muñoz P, Prem M. *Managers' Productivity and Recruitment in the Public Sector: The Case of School Principals*, Working Paper 1303. Toulouse: Toulouse School of Economics, 2022.
170. Organisation for Economic Co-operation and Development. *PISA 2022 Results: Factsheets United Kingdom*. Paris: OECD Publishing, 2023.
171. Högberg B. Is there a trade-off between achievement and wellbeing in education systems? New cross-country evidence. *Child Indicators Research*, 2023, 16: 2165–86.
172. Mason-Jones AJ, Sinclair D, Mathews C et al. School-based interventions for preventing HIV, sexually transmitted infections, and pregnancy in adolescents. *Cochrane Database of Systematic Reviews*, 2016, 11(11): CD006417.
173. Fletcher A, Bonell C, Sorhaindo A. 'We don't have no drugs education': the myth of universal drugs education in English secondary schools? *International Journal of Drug Policy*, 2010, 21(6): 452–8.
174. Durlak JA, Weissberg RP, Dymnicki AB. The impact of enhancing students' social and emotional learning: a meta-analysis of school-based universal interventions. *Child Development*, 2011, 82(1): 405–32.
175. Montero-Marin J, Allwood M, Ball S et al. School-based mindfulness training in early adolescence: what works, for whom and how in the MYRIAD trial? *Evidence Based Mental Health*, 2022, 25(3): 117–24.
176. Department for Education. *Relationships and Sex Education (RSE) and Health Education: Statutory Guidance on Relationships Education, Relationships and Sex Education (RSE) and Health Education*. London: Department for Education, 2019.
177. Andrews JL, Birrell L, Chapman C et al. Evaluating the effectiveness of a universal eHealth school-based prevention programme for depression and anxiety, and the moderating role of friendship network characteristics. *Psychological Medicine*, 2023, 53(11): 5042–51.
178. Stallard P, Phillips R, Montgomery AA et al. A cluster randomised controlled trial to determine the clinical effectiveness and cost-effectiveness of classroom-based cognitive-behavioural therapy (CBT) in reducing symptoms of depression in high-risk adolescents. *Health Technology Assessment*, 2013, 17(47): 1–109.

[179] Department of Health and Department for Education. *Transforming Children and Young People's Mental Health Provision: A Green Paper*. London: Department of Health and Department for Education, 2017.

[180] Cipriano C, Strambler MJ, Naples LH et al. The state of evidence for social and emotional learning: a contemporary meta-analysis of universal school-based SEL interventions. *Child Development*, 2023, 94(5): 1181–204.

[181] Kidger J, Turner N, Hollingworth W et al. An intervention to improve teacher well-being support and training to support students in UK high schools (the WISE study): a cluster randomised controlled trial. *PLoS Medicine*, 2021, 18(11): art e1003847. doi: 10.1371/journal.pmed.1003847

[182] Kuyken W, Blakemore SJ, Byford S et al. Mental health in adolescence: the role of schools-based social emotional teaching. *Journal of Mental Health*, 2023, 32(3): 537–40.

[183] Dishion TJ, McCord J, Poulin F. When interventions harm. *American Psychologist*, 1999, 54(9): 755–64.

[184] Wiggins M, Bonell C, Sawtell M et al. Health outcomes of youth development programme in England: prospective matched comparison study. *BMJ*, 2009, 339(b2534). doi: 10.1136/bmj.b2534

[185] Allen JP, Philliber S, Herrling S et al. Preventing teen pregnancy and academic failure: experimental evaluation of a deveolopmentally-based approach. *Child Development*, 1999, 64(4): 929–42.

[186] Bonell C, Jamal F, Melendez-Torres GJ et al. 'Dark logic' – theorising the harmful consequences of public health interventions. *Journal of Epidemiology and Community Health*, 2015, 69(1): 95–8.

[187] Foulkes L, Andrews JL. Are mental health awareness efforts contributing to the rise in reported mental health problems? A call to test the prevalence inflation hypothesis. *New Ideas in Psychology*, 2023, 69: art 101010. doi: 10.1016/j.newideapsych.2023.101010

[188] Guzman-Holst C, Zaneva M, Chessell C et al. Do antibullying interventions reduce internalizing symptoms? A systematic review, meta-analysis, and meta-regression exploring intervention components, moderators, and mechanisms. *Journal Child Psychol Psychiatry*, 2022, 63(12): 1454–65.

[189] Andrews JL, Birrell L, Chapman C et al. Evaluating the effectiveness of a universal eHealth school-based prevention programme for depression and anxiety, and the moderating role of friendship network characteristics. *Psychological Medicine*, 53(11): 5042–51.

[190] Tse ZWM, Emad S, Hasan MK et al. School-based cognitive-behavioural therapy for children and adolescents with social anxiety disorder and social anxiety symptoms: a systematic review. *PLoS One*, 2023, 18(3): art e0283329. doi: 10.1371/journal.pone.0283329

[191] Clarke A, Sorgenfrei M, Mulcahy J et al. *Adolescent Mental Health: A Systematic Review on the Effectiveness of School-Based Interventions.* London: Early Intervention Foundation, 2021.

[192] Wigelsworth M, Humphrey N, Lendrum A. A national evaluation of the impact of the secondary social and emotional aspects of learning (SEAL) programme. *Educational Psychology*, 2012, 32(2): 213–38.

[193] Mihalic S. The importance of implementation fidelity. *Emotional and Behavioral Disorders in Youth*, 2004, 4(4): 83–105.

[194] Ponsford R, Bragg S, Allen E et al. A school-based social-marketing intervention to promote sexual health in English secondary schools: the Positive Choices pilot cluster RCT. *Public Health Research*, 2021, 9(1): 1–189.

[195] Pound P, Denford S, Shucksmith J et al. What is best practice in sex and relationship education? A synthesis of evidence, including stakeholders' views. *BMJ Open*, 2017, 7: art e014791. doi:10.1136/bmjopen-2016-014791

[196] Herlitz L, MacIntyre H, Osborn T et al. The sustainability of public health interventions in schools: a systematic review. *Implementation Science*, 2020, 15(1): art 4. doi: 10.1186/s13012-019-0961-8

[197] Kuyken W, Ball S, Crane C et al. Effectiveness and cost-effectiveness of universal school-based mindfulness training compared with normal school provision in reducing risk of mental health problems and promoting well-being in adolescence: the MYRIAD cluster randomised controlled trial. *BMJ Evidence-Based Mental Health*, 2022. doi: 0.1136/ebmental-2021-300396

[198] Farahmand FK, Grant KE, Polo AJ et al. School-based mental health and behavioral programs for low-income, urban youth: a systematic and meta-analytic review. *Clinical Psychology*, 2011, 18(4): 372–90.

[199] Melendez-Torres GJ, Tancred T, Fletcher A et al. Does integrated academic and health education prevent substance use? Systematic review and meta-analyses. *Child: Care, Health & Development*, 2018, 44: 516–30.

[200] Weiss C. Nothing as practical as good theory: exploring theory-based evaluation for comprehensive community-based initiatives for children and families. In Connell J, Kubisch A, Schorr L et al (eds) *New Approaches to Evaluating Community Initiatives: Concepts, Methods and Contexts.* Washington, DC: Aspen Institute, 1995, pp 65–92.

[201] Bonell C, Fletcher A, Jamal F et al. Theories of how the school environment impacts on student health: systematic review and synthesis. *Health and Place*, 2013, 24: 242–9.

[202] Hawkins JD, Weiss JG. The social development model: an integrated approach to delinquency prevention. *Journal of Primary Prevention*, 1985, 6: 73–97.

203 Portes A. Social capital: its origins and applications in modern sociology. *Annual Review of Sociology*, 1998, 24: 1–24.

204 Coleman JS. Social capital in the creation of human capital. *The American Journal of Sociology*, 1988, 97(Supplement: Organizations and Institutions: Sociological and Economic Appraoches to the Analysis of Social Structure): S95–S120.

205 Markham WA, Aveyard P. A new theory of health promoting schools based on human functioning, school organisation and pedagogic practice. *Social Science & Medicine*, 2003, 56(6): 1209–20.

206 Bonell C, Fletcher A, Fitzgerald-Yau N et al. A pilot randomised controlled trial of the INCLUSIVE intervention for initiating change locally in bullying and aggression through the school environment: final report. *Health Technology Assessment*, 2013, 19(53): 1–109.

207 Bonell C, Allen E, Warren E et al. Modifying the secondary school environment to reduce bullying and aggression: the INCLUSIVE cluster RCT. *Public Health Research*, 2019, 7(18). doi: 10.3310/phr07180

208 Warren EBL, Opondo C, Allen E et al. Action groups as a participative strategy for leading whole-school health promotion: results on implementation from the INCLUSIVE trial in English secondary schools. *British Education Research Journal*, 2019, 45(5): 979–1000.

209 Fletcher A, Fitzgerald-Yau N, Wiggins M et al. Involving young people in changing their school environment to make it safer: findings from a process evaluation in English secondary schools. *Health Education*, 2015, 115(3/4): 322–38.

210 Thomson K, Hillier-Brown F, Todd A et al. The effects of public health policies on health inequalities in high-income countries: an umbrella review. *BMC Public Health*, 2018, 18(1): art 869. doi: 10.1186/s12889-018-5677-1

211 Bonell C, Dodd M, Allen E et al. Broader impacts of an intervention to transform school environments on student behaviour and school functioning: post hoc analyses from the INCLUSIVE cluster randomised controlled trial. *BMJ Open*, 2020, 10(5): art e031589. doi: 10.1136/bmjopen-2019-031589

212 Melendez-Torres GJ, Allen E, Viner R et al. Effects of a whole-school health intervention on clustered adolescent health risks: latent transition analysis of data from the INCLUSIVE trial. *Prevention Science*, 2022, 23(1): 1–9.

213 Ioannidis JP. Why most published research findings are false. *PLOS Medicine*, 2005, 2(8): art e124. doi: 10.1371/journal.pmed.0020124

214 Camerer CF, Dreber A, Forsell E et al. Evaluating replicability of laboratory experiments in economics. *Science*, 2016, 351(6280): 1433–36.

215 Ponsford R, Melendez-Torres GJ, Miners A et al. Whole-school interventions promoting student commitment to school to prevent substance use and violence, and improve educational attainment: a systematic review. *Public Health Research*, 2023, 12(2): 1–290.

216 Flay BR, Graumlich S, Segawa E et al. Effects of 2 prevention programs on high-risk behaviors among African American youth: a randomized trial. *Archives of Pediatrics & Adolescent Medicine*, 2004, 158(4): 377–84.

217 Flay B, Petraitis J. The theory of triadic influence: an integrative model of substance use. *Advances in Medical Sociology*, 1994, 4: 19–44.

218 Bond L, Butler H. The Gatehouse Project: a multi-level integrated approach to promoting wellbeing in schools. Draft chapter for NICE publication, 2008.

219 Patton G, Bond L, Carlin JB et al. Promoting social inclusion in schools: group-randomized trial of effects on student health risk behaviour and well-being. *American Journal of Public Health*, 2006, 96(9): 1582–7.

220 Hawkins JD, Catalano RF, Kosterman R et al. Preventing adolescent health-risk behaviors by strengthening protection during childhood. *Archives of Pediatrics & Adolescent Medicine*, 1999, 153(3): 226–34.

221 Hill KG, Bailey JA, Hawkins JD et al. The onset of STI diagnosis through age 30: results from the Seattle Social Development Project Intervention. *Prevention Science*, 2014, 15(supp 1): S19–S32.

222 Van Ryzin MJ, Roseth CJ. Cooperative learning in middle school: a means to improve peer relations and reduce victimization, bullying, and related outcomes. *Journal of Educational Psychology*, 2018, 110: 1192–201.

223 Van Ryzin MJ, Roseth CJ. Cooperative learning effects on peer relations and alcohol use in middle school. *Journal of Applied Developmental Psychology*, 2019, 64: art 101059. doi: 10.1016/j.appdev.2019.101059

224 Van Ryzin MJ, Roseth CJ. Effects of cooperative learning on peer relations, empathy, and bullying in middle school. *Aggressive Behavior*, 2019, 45: 643–51.

225 Van Ryzin MJ, Roseth CJ. Peer influence processes as mediators of effects of a middle school substance use prevention program. *Addictive Behaviours*, 2018, 85: 180–5.

226 Devries KM, Knight L, Child JC et al. The Good School Toolkit for reducing physical violence from school staff to primary school students: a cluster-randomised controlled trial in Uganda. *The Lancet Global Health*, 2015, 3(7): e378–e386.

227 Dzewaltowski DA, Estabrooks PA, Welk G et al. Healthy youth places: a randomized controlled trial to determine the effectiveness of facilitating adult and youth leaders to promote physical activity and fruit and vegetable consumption in middle schools. *Health Education & Behavior*, 2009, 36(3): 583–600.

[228] Shinde, Weiss HA, Varghese B et al. Promoting school climate and health outcomes with the SEHER multi-component secondary school intervention in Bihar, India: a cluster-randomised controlled trial. *The Lancet*, 2018, 392: 2465–77.

[229] Singla DR, Shinde S, Patton G et al. the mediating effect of school climate on adolescent mental health: findings from a randomized controlled trial of a school-wide intervention. *Journal of Adolescent Health*, 2021, 69(1): 90–9.

[230] Goyer JP, Cohen GL, Cook JE et al. Targeted identity-safety interventions cause lasting reductions in discipline citations among negatively stereotyped boys. *Journal of Personality and Social Psychology*, 2019, 117(2): 229–59.

[231] Borman GD, Rozek CS, Pyne J et al. Reappraising academic and social adversity improves middle school students' academic achievement, behavior, and well-being. *Proceedings of the National Academy of Sciences*, 2019, 116(33): 16286–91.

[232] Okonofua JA, Pauneskua D, Walton GM. Brief intervention to encourage empathic discipline cuts suspension rates in half among adolescents. *Proceedings of the National Academy of Sciences*, 2016, 113(19): 5221–6.

[233] Okonofua JA, Goyer JP, Lindsay CA et al. A scalable empathic-mindset intervention reduces group disparities in school suspensions. *Scientific Advances*, 2022, 8(12): art eabj0691. doi: 10.1126/sciadv.abj069

[234] Pyne P, Borman GD. Replicating a scalable intervention that helps students reappraise academic and social adversity during the transition to middle school. *Journal of Research on Educational Effectiveness*, 2020, 13(4): 652–78.

[235] Williams CL, Hirschi Q, Sublett KV et al. A brief social belonging intervention improves academic outcomes for minoritized high school students. *Motivation Science*, 2020, 6(4): 423–3.

[236] Walton GM, Cohen GL. A brief social-belonging intervention improves academic and health outcomes of minority students. *Science*, 2011, 331(6023): 1447–51.

[237] Brady ST, Cohen GL, Jarvis SN et al. A brief social-belonging intervention in college improves adult outcomes for Black Americans. *Science Advances*, 2020, 6: art eaay3689. doi: 10.1126/sciadv.aay3689

[238] Okonofua JA, Walton GM, Eberhardt JL. A vicious cycle: a social-psychological account of extreme racial disparities in school discipline. *Perspectives on Psychological Science*, 2016, 11: 381–98.

[239] Cochrane A. *Effectiveness and Efficiency: Random Reflections on Health Services*. London: Nuffield Provincial Hospitals Trust, 1972.

240. Melendez-Torres GJ, Ponsford R, Falconer J et al. Whole-school interventions promoting student commitment to school to prevent substance use and violence: a systematic review. *Public Health*, 2023, 221: 190–7.
241. Ponsford R, Falconer J, Melendez-Torres GJ et al. What factors influence implementation of whole-school interventions aiming to promote student commitment to school to prevent substance use and violence? Systematic review and synthesis of process evaluations. *BMC Public Health*, 2022, 22(1): art 2148. doi: 10.1186/s12889-022-14544-4
242. Sadjadi M, Blanchard L, Brulle S et al. Barriers and facilitators to the implementation of Health-Promoting School programmes targeting bullying and violence: a systematic review. *Health Education Research*, 2021, 36(5): 581–99.
243. Warren E, Melendez-Torres GJ, Viner RM et al. Using qualitative research within a realist trial to build theory about how context and mechanisms interact to generate outcomes: findings from the INCLUSIVE trial of a whole-school health intervention. *Trials*, 2020, 21: art 774. doi: 10.1186/s13063-020-04688-2
244. Melendez-Torres GJ, Warren E, Viner R et al. Moderated mediation analyses to assess intervention mechanisms for impacts on victimisation, psycho-social problems and mental wellbeing: evidence from the INCLUSIVE realist randomized trial. *Social Science and Medicine*, 2021, 279: art 113984. doi: 0.1016/j.socscimed.2021.113984
245. Bonell C, Taylor T, Berry V et al. Re-orienting systematic reviews to rigorously examine what works, for whom and how: example of a realist systematic review of school-based prevention of dating and gender violence. *Research Synthesis Methods*, 2023, 14(4): 582–95.
246. Ofsted. *Review of Sexual Abuse in Schools and Colleges*. London: Ofsted, 2021.
247. Ponsford R, Meiksin R, Allen E et al. The Positive Choices trial: study protocol for a Phase-III RCT trial of a whole-school social-marketing intervention to promote sexual health and reduce health inequalities. *Trials*, 2021, 22(1): art 818. doi: 10.1186/s13063-021-05793-6
248. Peterson AJ, Donze M, Allen E et al. Effects of interventions addressing school environments or educational assets on adolescent sexual health: systematic review and meta-analysis. *International Perspectives on Sexual and Reproductive Health*, 2018, 44(3): 11–131.
249. Marmot MG. *Fair Society, Healthy Lives. The Marmot Review. Strategic Review of Health Inequalities in England post-2010*. London: The Marmot Review, 2010.
250. Ginsburg-Block MD, Rohrbeck CA, Fantuzzo JW. A meta-analytic review of social, self-concept, and behavioral outcomes of peer-assisted learning. *Journal of Educational Psychology*, 2006, 98: 732–49.

251 Murray NG, Low BJ, Hollis C et al. Coordinated school health programs and academic achievement: a systematic review of the literature. *Journal of School Health*, 2007, 77: 589–600.

252 UNESCO. *Survey on National Education Responses to COVID-19 School Closures*, 2021. Available at: http://tcg.uis.unesco.org/survey-education-covid-school-closures/ (Accessed 15 April 2024).

253 Ortega Pacheco Y, Barrero Toncel V. The impact of school closure on children's well-being during the COVID-19 pandemic. *Asian Journal of Psychiatry*, 2022, 67: art 102957. doi: 10.1016/j.ajp.2021.102957

254 Mazrekaj D, De Witte K. The impact of school closures on learning and mental health of children: lessons from the COVID-19 pandemic. *Perspectives on Psychological Science*, 2023, 19(4): 686–93.

255 Newlove-Delgado T, Russell AE, Mathews F et al. Annual research review: the impact of Covid-19 on psychopathology in children and young people worldwide: systematic review of studies with pre- and within-pandemic data. *Journal of Child Psychology & Psychiatry*, 2023, 64(4): 611–40.

256 Education Endowment Foundation. *The Impact of COVID-19 on Learning: A Review of the Evidence*. London: Education Endowment Foundation, 2022.

257 UNESCO. *Global Monitoring of School Closures Caused by COVID-19*, 2023. Available at: https://covid19.uis.unesco.org/global-monitoring-school-closures-covid19/country-dashboard/ (Accessed 15 April 2024).

258 NHS Digital. *Mental Health of Children and Young People in England 2022 – Wave 3 Follow Up to the 2017 Survey*. London: NHS Digital, 2022.

259 Andrew A, Cattan S, Costa Dias M, et al. *Learning during the Lockdown: Real-Time Data on Children's Experiences during Home Learning*, IFS Briefing Note 288. London: Institute for Fiscal Studies, 2020.

260 Department for Education. 2022. *Pupil Absence in Schools in England*. London: Department for Education, 2024.

261 Burgess S, Crawford C, Macmillan L. *Assessing the Role of Grammar Schools in Promoting Social Mobility*, Working Paper 17–09. London: Department of Quantitative Social Science, University College London, 2017.

262 Burgess S, Dickson M, Macmillan L. Do selective schooling systems increase inequality? *Oxford Economic Papers*, 2020, 72(1): 1–24.

263 Titmuss RM. *Essays on the Welfare State*. London: Unwin University Books, 1963.

264 Schleicher A. *Programme for International Student Assessment Insights and Interpretations PISA 2022*. Paris: OECD Publishing, 2023.

265 Gibbons S, Machin S, Silva O. Valuing school quality using boundary discontinuities. *Journal of Urban Economics*, 2013, 75: 15–28.

266. Shackleton N, Allen E, Bevilacqua L et al. Associations between socio-economic status (including school- and pupil-level interactions) and student perceptions of school environment and health in English secondary schools. *British Educational Research Journal*, 2018, 44(5): 748–62.
267. Stasz C, van Stolk C. *The Use of Lottery Systems in School Admissions*. London: Sutton Trust, 2007.
268. National Foundation for Educational Research. *An Analysis of the Demand for Skills in the Labour Market in 2035*, Working Paper 3. Slough: National Foundation for Educational Research, 2023.
269. Tony Blair Institute for Global Change. *Ending the Big Squeeze on Skills: How to Futureproof Education in England*. London: TBIGC, 2022.
270. Niemann D, Martens K. Soft governance by hard fact? The OECD as a knowledge broker in education policy. *Global Social Policy*, 2018, 18(3): 267–83.
271. Popper K. *The Open Society and Its Enemies, Vol 2: Hegel and Marx*. London: Routledge and Kegan Paul, 1945.
272. Walker M, Nelson J, Bradshaw S et al. *Teachers' Engagement with Research: What Do We Know? A Research Briefing*. London: Education Endowment Foundation, 2019.
273. Coldwell M, Greany T, Higgins S et al. *Evidence-Informed Teaching: An Evaluation of Progress in England*. London: Department for Education, 2017.
274. Pegram J, Watkins RC, Hoerger M et al. Assessing the range and evidence-base of interventions in a typical school cluster. *Review of Education*, 2022, 10(1): art e3336. doi: 10.1002/rev3.3336
275. Development OfECa. *Effective Teacher Policies: Insights from PISA*. Paris: OECD Publishing, 2018.
276. Department for Education. *Initial Teacher Training Census*. London: Department for Education, 2023.
277. House of Commons Library. *Teacher Recruitment and Retention in England*, Research Briefing 07222. London: House of Commons, 2022.
278. Sibieta L. *The Teacher Labour Market in England: Shortages, Subject Expertise and Incentives*. London: Education Policy Institute, 2018.
279. Slater H, Davies NM, Burgess S. Do teachers matter? measuring the variation in teacher effectiveness in England. *Oxford Bulletin of Economics and Statistics*, 2012, 74(5): 629–45.
280. Papay J, Kraft M. Productivity returns to experience in the teacher labor market: methodological challenges and new evidence on long-term career improvement. *Journal of Public Economics*, 2015, 130: 105–19.
281. Leigh A. Teacher pay and teacher aptitude. *Economics of Education Review*, 2012, 31(3): 41–53.

[282] Jerrim J, Sims S, Taylor H et al. How does the mental health and wellbeing of teachers compare to other professions? Evidence from eleven survey datasets. *Review of Education*, 2020, 8(3): 659–89.

[283] Jerrim J, Sims S, Taylor H et al. Has the mental health and wellbeing of teachers in England changed over time? New evidence from three datasets. *Oxford Review of Education*, 2021, 47(6): 805–25.

[284] Gibbons S, McNally S, Viarengo M. Does additional spending help urban schools? An evaluation using boundary discontinuities. *Journal of the European Economic Association*, 2018, 16(5): 1618–68.

[285] Ofsted. *Independent Review of Teachers' Professional Development in Schools: Phase 1 Findings*. London: Office for Standards in Education, Children's Services and Skills, 2024.

[286] Machin S, McNally S, Viarengo M. Changing how literacy is taught: evidence on synthetic phonics. *American Economic Journal: Economic Policy*, 2018, 10(2): 217–41.

[287] Scrivener R, Morrell C, Baker R et al. *Principles for Best Practice in Clinical Audit*. Radcliffe Medical Press: Abingdon, 2002.

[288] Burgess S, Rawal S, Taylor ES. Teacher peer observation and student test scores: evidence from a field experiment in English secondary schools. *Journal of Labor Economics*, 2021, 39(4): 1155–86.

Index

A

Aban Aya (intervention) (US) 68
abuse 14, 15, 16–17, 24–5, 83, 84 *see also* harassment; violence
Academies Act 2010 35
actions groups *see* interventions
activity *see* physical activity
admissions 89–90
adolescence 22–23 *see also* students
alcohol use 25, 31, 32, 48, 65
Allen, Liz 64–5
anxiety (toxic mechanism of)
  author's overview of 2
  education policy on, impacts of 40–1
  failure, fear of 15–16
  health outcomes of 16–19, 19–21, 28
  students on 16, 40
  trends in 28–9, 31–2
  see also mental health
Arai, Lisa 10
arts 40, 89, 93, 96
attainment
  education policy and 36–8, 91, 93, 94
  factors that affect 25, 30, 43, 72, 86, 87, 89
  focus on 8, 9, 10, 31, 47, 66
  trends in 41, 88

B

before-and-after comparisons *see* quasi-experimental studies
Belgium 31
belonging *see* lack of belonging (toxic mechanism of)
Bond, Lyndal 56, 69
boundaries 53–4, 58
boys *see* male students
bullying
  cyberbullying 25, 66
  educational disengagement and 30
  fear/anxiety and 32
  interventions for 70, 71, 73–4, 83, 84–5, 97
  lack of belonging and 31
  Learning Together intervention and 56, 58, 64, 65–6, 80–1
  prevalence of 24–5, 96
  students on 14

C

Callaghan, James 34
cannabis use 8, 9, 13, 17–19, 25–6
cigarettes *see* smoking
citizenship education 54, 89, 98

class-based identities 9
class inequalities 9
cognitive behavioural therapy 42, 43, 46, 97
Cooperative Learning (intervention) (US) 70
COVID-19 pandemic 4, 87, 88
curriculum 8, 34, 39, 54, 58–9, 84, 90–1
  see also national curriculum
cyberbullying 25, 66

D

dating violence 25, 83–4
diet 26, 29, 32, 96
disengagement *see* educational disengagement (toxic mechanism of)
diversity in schools 89–90, 95
drinking *see* alcohol use
drug use
  cannabis use 8, 9, 13, 17–19, 25–6
  educational disengagement and 9–10, 30
  fear/anxiety and 32
  lack of belonging and 31
  rates of in young people 26
  for safety 17–19
  see also substance use

E

early pregnancy *see* pregnancy
eating *see* diet
EBacc (English Baccalaureate) 36, 91
Education (Schools) Act 1992 34
educational disengagement (toxic mechanism of)
  author's overview of 2, 7
  education policy on, impacts of 39
  and human functioning and school organisation theory 52–4
  interventions for 72–3
  and risk behaviours 8–10, 28
  for safety 19
  students on 7–8
  trends in 28–9, 30–1
educational engagement
  impacts of 7
  and risk behaviours 10
Education Endowment Foundation 36, 39, 64, 92–3, 94
education policy
  changes to, author's recommended 89–93
  existing, what to keep in 87–8
  impacts of 4, 37–8, 96
  toxic mechanisms, impacts of on 39–41
  in United Kingdom 33–6
  in United States 36–7

122

Index

Education Reform Act 34
Education (School Teacher Appraisal) Regulations 1991 34
engagement *see* educational engagement
England
  attainment trends in 41
  COVID-19 lockdowns in 87
  cyberbullying in 25
  education policy in 35–6, 37–8, 90, 91
  obesity trends in 26
  substance use trends in 25, 26
  teachers in 93
  see also Learning Together (intervention)
English Baccalaureate (EBacc) 36, 91
Everyone's Invited initiative 84
Every Student Succeeds Act (US) 37
exercise *see* physical activity
experimental studies 50

F

fear (toxic mechanism of)
  author's overview of 2
  education policy on, impacts of 40–1
  health outcomes of 16–19, 19–21, 28
  safety, due to lack of 14–15
  students on 13, 40
  teachers on 14
  trends in 31–2
female students
  on anxiety 16
  on bullying 14
  diet and physical activity trends 26–7, 89
  educational disengagement of 7–8
  harassment of 14, 15, 16, 26
  'hyper girls' 7–8, 9–10, 20, 89–90
  interventions on, effectiveness of 44, 65, 68, 83
  mental health of 23, 87
  on risk behaviours 9–10, 17–19
  risk behaviours of 9–10
  self-medication 20
  on self-medication 20
  on sense of belonging 12–13
  sexual health trends 26
  substance use trends 25–6
  violence trends 25
Finland 31, 37, 93, 94
Flay, Brian 68, 69
Fletcher, Adam 16–17, 19, 20

G

Gatehouse Project (intervention) (Australia) 69
gender-based harassment 14
gender-based violence 83, 84
Germany 31, 89
girls *see* female students
Good School Toolkit (intervention) (Uganda) 70–1

H

harassment 14, 15, 16, 26
health interventions *see* interventions
health outcomes
  author's overview of 1
  of educational disengagement 10
  of fear and anxiety 16–19, 19–21, 28
  interventions 70–2
  schools on, impacts of 27–32
  trends in 29–30
healthy eating *see* diet
Healthy Youth Places (intervention) (US) 71
House of Lords 90
human functioning and school organisation theory 52–4, 58, 65
Humphrys, John 45
'hyper girls' 7–8, 9–10, 20, 89–90

I

identities
  class-based identity 9
  collective identity 9, 40, 72
  cultural identity 9
  development of students' 2, 7, 8–9, 23, 54
  'safe' identity 19
The Importance of Teaching 36
India 71–2, 82, 86
individualisation 11, 23, 40
inequalities
  class inequalities 9
  economic inequalities 85
  health inequalities 2, 24, 25, 27
  socioeconomic/ethnic inequalities 24, 38
interventions
  action groups 55–6, 59–60, 61, 76, 79–80
  author's overview of 1, 42, 97
  author's recommendations for 85–6, 97–8
  comparison of effectiveness in different schools 78–81, 82–3
  delivery of 46–7, 58–9, 78
  evaluation of, methods of 63
  harmful effects of 43–5
  health outcomes interventions 70–2
  impacts of 3–4, 42, 47–8
  implementation of 78–81
  mental health interventions 42, 45–6, 66–7, 69
  risk behaviours interventions 68, 69–70
  systematic reviews of 74–6
  for teachers 73
  for toxic mechanisms 72–3
  whole-school interventions 75, 83–4, 86
  see also Learning Together (intervention)

J

Jamal, Farah 10, 15
Japan 37, 93

L

Labour government 34, 35, 39, 46, 87–8, 91
lack of belonging (toxic mechanism of)
  author's overview of 2, 11
  education policy and 40, 89
  health outcomes of 28
  and human functioning and school organisation theory 52–4
  interventions for 72–3
  students on 12–13
  trends in 28–9, 31
league tables 4, 34, 35, 36, 37–8, 88
Learning Together (intervention)
  action groups 55–6, 59–60, 61, 79–80
  author's overview of 54–5
  delivery of 78
  effectiveness of 64–6
  evaluation of 62–4, 79–81
  external facilitator for 55, 57, 60–1
  needs assessments 55, 60
  restorative practice 56–7, 61–2, 80–1
  social and emotional learning 57, 58–9
  theory of change 57–8
Learning Together for Mental Health (intervention) 66–7
Learning Together Primary Schools (intervention) 67

M

male students
  fear/anxiety trends in 32
  harassment by 14
  harassment of 26
  interventions on, effectiveness of 65, 68, 72, 80, 83
  physical activity trends 27, 89
  on risk behaviours for safety 17
  substance use trends 25–6
  violence trends 25
marketisation 38
mechanisms *see* toxic mechanisms
mental health
  interventions 42, 45–6, 66–7, 69
  toxic mechanisms on, impacts of 28
  young people, trends in 23–4, 29, 31, 32, 87
Money to Burn (intervention) 48

N

national curriculum 34, 35, 36, 39, 88, 90–1, 95, 98
National Foundation for Educational Research 90–1
neoliberalism 38
No Child Left Behind (NCLB) Act 2002 (US) 37
Northern Ireland 35, 38

O

observational studies 49–50
Office for Standards in Education, Children's Services and Skills (Ofsted) 34, 36, 84, 93
Organisation for Economic Co-operation and Development (OECD) 37, 88, 91, 93

P

Palmer, Sue 15–16
pandemic *see* COVID-19 pandemic
Patton, George 68, 69
Paulle, Bowen 13, 16
pedagogy 91–3, 95, 98
performance metrics 37, 40, 91, 95, 98
physical activity
  interventions 71, 76–7
  sense of belonging and 28, 31, 89
  trends in 26–7, 29, 96
  see also sports
physical harassment 26
PISA (Programme for International Student Assessment) 91–2
Plastered (intervention) 48
policy *see* education policy
Positive Choices (intervention) 84
pregnancy 10, 26, 27, 43–4
prevalence inflation hypothesis 46
Programme for International Student Assessment (PISA) 91–2
Project Respect (intervention) 84
psychological abuse 25
Putnam, Robert 11, 52

Q

qualitative research
  author's overview of 3, 6
  on educational disengagement 7–10
  on fear and anxiety 13–16, 16–21
  on Learning Together intervention 58–62, 79–81
  sense of belonging, on lack of 11–13
quantitative research
  author's overview of 6
  health, impacts of school on 27–32
  on Learning Together intervention 81
  mental health in adolescents 23–4
quasi-experimental studies 43–5, 50, 63, 69–70

R

randomised controlled trials 62–4, 69, 71–2, 73, 91–2
reframing school provision 54, 58
relationship violence 25, 83–4
replication studies 68, 73

Index

research *see* experimental studies; observational studies; qualitative research; quantitative research; quasi-experimental studies; randomised controlled trials; replication studies; systematic reviews
risk behaviours
 author's overview of 1
 educational disengagement and 8–10
 interventions 68, 69–70
 for safety 16–19
 schools on, impacts of 27–32
 trends in 29–30, 96

S

safety, risk behaviours for 16–19
school provision, reframing of 54, 58
schools
 benefits of 2–3
 education policy in, history of 33–6
 intervention effectiveness, comparison of 78–81, 82–3
 league tables 4, 34, 35, 36, 37–8, 88
 see also attainment; education policy; interventions; qualitative research; students; teachers; toxic mechanisms
Scotland 25, 31, 35, 38, 66
Scotland Act 1998 35
Seattle Social Development Project (US) 69–70
SEHER (intervention) (India) 71–2, 82, 86
self-harm 19–20
self-medication 2, 19, 20
sense of belonging *see* lack of belonging (toxic mechanism of)
sexual abuse 15, 25, 84
sexual harassment 14, 15, 16, 26
sexual health
 educational disengagement and 30
 interventions for 72, 74, 84–5
 toxic mechanisms on, impacts of 28
 young people, trends in 26, 32, 96
Singapore 93, 94
smoking 9, 25–6, 28, 30–1, 48, 65 *see also* drug use
social capital theory 52
social development model 51–2
socialisation 1, 53
social media 24–5, 80–1
South Korea 93
sports 12, 40, 89, 96, 98 *see also* physical activity
street styles 8, 9, 10, 17
Student Belonging (intervention) (US) 72, 73, 82
students
 in action groups 79–80
 on anxiety 16, 40

on educational disengagement 7–8
on Learning Together intervention 59–60, 62
on restorative practice 80–1
see also female students; male students
substance use
 alcohol use 25, 31, 32, 48, 65
 fear/anxiety and 31–2
 interventions for, review of 75–6
 rates of in young people 25–6, 96
 for safety 17–19
 see also drug use
systematic reviews 74–6, 78, 82–3, 97

T

Teacher Empathetic Discipline (intervention) (US) 73, 82
teachers
 on action groups 79, 80
 classroom focus of 14–15
 on educational disengagement 19
 on fear 14
 interventions by, delivery of 47
 interventions for 73
 on Learning Together intervention 59, 60–1, 62
 recruitment and retention of 93
 on self-medication 19–20
 status of 94
 on time with students 20–1
 training of 94
teen pregnancy *see* pregnancy
theories *see* human functioning and school organisation theory; social capital theory; social development model; theories of change
theories of change 57–8
tobacco *see* smoking
Toxic Childhood (Palmer) 15–16
toxic mechanisms
 author's overview of 2
 education policy on, impacts of 39–41
 health outcomes, impacts of on 28
 observational studies of 49–50
 see also anxiety (toxic mechanism of); educational disengagement (toxic mechanism of); fear (toxic mechanism of); health outcomes; lack of belonging (toxic mechanism of); risk behaviours

U

Uganda 70–1
United Kingdom (UK)
 attainment trends in 41, 88
 bullying trends in 24–5, 32
 education policy in 33–6, 37–8, 87–8
 mental health in 23–4
 physical activity trends in 27
 sexual health trends in 26, 32

substance use trends in 25, 32
teachers in 93, 94
toxic mechanisms trends in 28–9, 31–2
violence trends in 24–5, 84
United States (US)
  Aban Aya intervention 68
  Cooperative Learning intervention 70
  education policy in 36–7
  Healthy Youth Places intervention 71
  Seattle Social Development Project 69–70
  sexual health trends in 26, 30
  Student Belonging intervention 72, 73, 82
  Teacher Empathetic Discipline intervention 73, 82
  toxic mechanisms trends in 10, 14–15, 30, 31, 32
  violence trends in 18

V

vaping 25
verbal harassment 26
violence
  author's overview of 83
  dating and relationship violence 25, 83–4
  educational disengagement and 8, 9, 30
  gender-based violence 83, 84
  interventions for 70–1, 72, 73–4, 75–6, 80–1, 82–5
  for safety 17, 18
  in schools 13–14, 41
  young people, experienced by 24–5, 32
  see also bullying

W

Wales 25, 35, 37–8, 66, 88, 92
weed *see* cannabis use
wellness interventions *see* interventions
Willis, Paul 9

Y

young people *see* health outcomes; interventions; mental health; risk behaviours; sexual health; students; substance use; violence
Young People's Development Programme 43–5

www.ingramcontent.com/pod-product-compliance
Lightning Source LLC
Chambersburg PA
CBHW071211070526
44584CB00019B/3001